2
Christ Our Life

God Cares for Us

AUTHORS

Sisters of Notre Dame of Chardon, Ohio

Sister Mary Theresa Betz, S.N.D.
Sister Mary Kathleen Glavich, S.N.D.
Sister Jeanne Mary Nieminen, S.N.D.

THEOLOGICAL ADVISOR

Sister Agnes Cunningham, S.S.C.M.

CONSULTANTS

Reverend Monsignor Joseph M. Champlin
Reverend Monsignor Joseph T. Moriarty

GENERAL EDITOR

Sister Mary Kathleen Glavich, S.N.D.

LOYOLAPRESS.

CHICAGO

Nihil Obstat: Sister Donna Marie Bradesca, O.S.U, M.S.E., D.Min., Censor Deputatus
Imprimatur: The Reverend Monsignor Joseph T. Moriarty, M.A., Bishop of Cleveland
Given at Cleveland, Ohio, on 5 March 1996

The *Nihil Obstat* and *Imprimatur* are official declarations that a book or pamphlet is free of doctrinal or moral error. No implication is contained therein that those who have granted the *Nihil Obstat* and *Imprimatur* agree with the contents, opinions, or statements expressed.

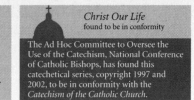

Christ Our Life
found to be in conformity

The Ad Hoc Committee to Oversee the Use of the Catechism, National Conference of Catholic Bishops, has found this catechetical series, copyright 1997 and 2002, to be in conformity with the *Catechism of the Catholic Church.*

Dedicated to St. Julie Billiart, foundress of the Sisters of Notre Dame, in gratitude for her inspiration and example

Acknowledgments

This present revision of the Christ Our Life series is the work of countless people. In particular, we acknowledge and thank the following for their roles in the project:

- The Sisters of Notre Dame who supported the production of the Christ Our Life series, especially Sister Mary Joell Overman, S.N.D.; Sister Mary Frances Murray, S.N.D.; and Sister Mary Margaret Hess, S.N.D.
- The Sisters of Notre Dame and others who over the past twenty years have shaped, written, and edited editions of the Christ Our Life series, in particular Sister Mary de Angelis Bothwell, S.N.D., the former editor
- Those who worked on different stages involved in producing this edition, especially Sister Mary Julie Boehnlein, S.N.D.; Sister Linda Marie Gecewicz, S.N.D.; Sister Mary Beth Gray, S.N.D.; Sister Joanmarie Harks, S.N.D.; Sister Rita Mary Harwood, S.N.D.; Sister Mary Nanette Herman, S.N.D.; Sister Mary Andrew Miller, S.N.D.; Sister Mary Agnes O'Malley, S.N.D.; Sister Mary Catherine Rennecker, S.N.D.; and Sister Mary St. Jude Weisensell, S.N.D.
- Those catechists, directors of religious education, priests, parents, students, and others who responded to surveys, returned evaluation forms, wrote letters, or participated in interviews to help improve the series
- The personnel at Loyola Press who helped make our vision a reality

Scripture selections are taken from *The New American Bible,* copyright © 1991, 1986, 1970 by the Confraternity of Christian Doctrine, Washington, D.C., and are used by license of copyright owner. All rights reserved.

Excerpts from the English translation of *The Roman Missal* ©1973, International Committee on English in the Liturgy, Inc. (ICEL); excerpts from the English translation of *Rite of Penance* © 1974, ICEL; excerpts from the English translation of *A Book of Prayers* © 1982, ICEL; excerpts from the English translation of *Book of Blessings* © 1988, ICEL. All rights reserved.

All attempts possible have been made to contact the publisher for cited works in this book.

Photographs

© **Artville LLC.** (p. 116C left); © **Sister Mary Julie Boehlein, S.N.D** (p. 151); © **Don Bosco Mulitmedia** (p. 122); © **Gabriel Bouys/AFP Worldwide** (p. 117); © **Christie's Images/SuperStock, Inc.** (p. 61); © **Cleo Freelance Photography** (pp. 21 top right, 34 top right, 70, 93 right bottom, 97, 109); © **Digital Stock Crop.** (pp. 14, 21 middle right, 32 top right, 34 top left, 36 top right, 37 top, 55 top left and bottom, 93 right middle); © **EyeWire** (p. 32 bottom); © **Charlene Faris** (p. 120 top right); © **Myrleen Ferguson/PhotoEdit** (pp. 32 middle, 55 top right, 62, 85, 96, 134A); © **Tony Freeman/PhotoEdit** (p. 25); © **Brett Froomer/The Image Bank** (p. 119); © **Brent Jones/Merrill Chicago** (p. 63 top); © **George A. Lane** (pp. 86 top, 91, 135); © **L'Osservatore Romano** (p. 18 bottom); © **Sidney McCarten/PhotoEdit** (p. 34 bottom right); © **Norma Morrison** (p. 34 bottom left); © **Jonathon Nourak/PhotoEdit** (p. 42A); © **Alan Oddie/PhotoEdit** (p. 120 top left and bottom); ©**PhotoDisc, Inc.** (pp. 2, 4, 8, 21 left, 36 left and bottom right, 38 bottom, 44, 49, 54, 56, 58, 63 bottom, 86 bottom, 88 bottom, 93 right top and left, 112, 116C right); © **Zdenek J. Pivecka** (pp. 16, 17, 105 right); **Eugene D. Plaisted, O.S.C./Crosiers** (pp. i, iii, 9, 18 top, 43, 47 top left and top right, 80 left and bottom right, 105 right); © **James L. Shaffer** (pp. 68A, 134C); © **SuperStock, Inc.** (pp. 38 middle, 76); © **Suzanne Szasz/Photo Researchers, Inc.** (p. 37 bottom); © **Wheater/Maryknoll** (p. 38 top); © **W. P. Wittman Limited** (pp. 1, 21 bottom right, 24, 27, 47 bottom, 71, 80 top right, 83, 88 top, 100, 104, 105 left, 108, 111, 118, 131); © **David Wolff-Young/PhotoEdit** (p. 32 top left).

Artwork

Diana Bush (pp. 74, 140); **Don Dyen** (pp. 46, 66, 76, 119, 136, 141); **Len Ebert** (pp. 5 top, 13, 23, 28, 33, 45, 50, 68, 82, 84, 87, 90, 103, 114, 121, 122, 126); **Larry Frederick/John Walter & Associates** (p. 68D); **George Hamblin/Steven Edsey & Sons** (pp. 68B, 68C, 134D Jesus inset); **Jack Jasper** (p. 12); **Diane Johnson** (pp. 51 bottom, 64, 85, 89, 92, 99, 128); **Sandra Kessler** (p. 71); **Laser Type and Graphics** (pp. 3, 9, 14, 18, 19, 22, 27, 29, 32, 33 heart, 37, 38, 39, 41, 56, 57, 69, 98, 101, 116, 123, 127, 137 top); **Laurie Marks** (pp. 10 left, 40, 94); **Proof Positive/Farrowlyne Assoc., Inc.** (pp. 5 bottom, 10 right, 42D, 60, 75, 79 color type, 81, 95, 116A, 116D, 134D church, 137 bottom right); **Sally Schaedler** (pp. 6, 7, 8, 11, 15, 20, 26, 31, 42D, 51 top, 52, 65, 72–73, 77, 78–79, 106–107, 124–125, 138–139); **Robert Voigts** (p. 94).

Artwork *(Perforated Section)*

Ralph Smith, except Easter basket and eggs by **Faye Zalecki/Z Graphics**; Scripture Prayer Booklet: **Diana Bush** (pp. 2, 4, 5, 6, 7, 8, 9, 11); **Diane Johnson** (pp. 1 border, 12); **Laser Type and Graphics** (p. 3); Punchouts by **Diana Bush,** except finger puppets and Zacchaeus/tree by **Len Ebert;** "God's Top 10" by **Robert Voigts.**

design by Donald Kye.
t © Eugene D. Plaisted, O.S.C./Crosiers.
03 04 05 06 6 5 4 3 2 1

LOYOLAPRESS.

3441 N. ASHLAND AVENUE
CHICAGO, ILLINOIS 60657
(800) 621-1008

CONTENTS

2

Notes to Parents

Goals of the Program

God Cares for Us prepares your child to celebrate the Sacrament of Reconciliation (Penance) and the Eucharist. Your child learns many signs of God's loving care and practical ways to use his or her talents to share God's love with others. The program leads the children to respond joyfully to God's call to give themselves in love to him and others.

Format Makes It a Family Program

A separate Reconciliation booklet (Jesus Gives Me His Peace) and a Mass booklet (Jesus Gives Himself) will help you prepare your child for the sacraments. Two family celebrations in this book are immediate preparation for your child's celebration of Reconciliation (page 69) and First Communion (page 116).

Review with your child the text and booklet pages (listed in the Family Corner at the end of each chapter). In class your child will mark the box in this corner with an X when he or she has completed the material.

Each unit in this book begins with a summary of the message to be presented in class. Each chapter highlights one aspect of the message presented each week. The Family Corners summarize the chapter's message and suggest related family activities under four topics.

Read Gives a scriptural reading that can be done by a parent or older child in the family.

Discuss Opens discussion that applies the Scripture reading to daily life.

Pray Sums up the message for the week in a short prayer of the heart, which all can say daily. This prayer might be printed and posted on the refrigerator or a mirror, or added to meal prayers or other family prayers.

Do Provides ideas for sharing at meals, playing games, and enjoying family activities related to the message of the chapter. Storybooks available in public libraries are suggested.

Beginning with the second unit, each unit ends with Family Feature pages that suggest a family custom and provide review activities.

Educating Your Child to Live in Christ Jesus

Even young children should learn that membership in the Church demands a belief in Jesus and his Church and a desire to live according to his teachings. This checklist is for you and your child's catechist to discuss periodically with your child. When your child and you agree that the response is part of your child's daily life, check the respective box.

I Love God and Others

I pray to God:

❑ in the morning

❑ at mealtimes

❑ before I go to bed

❑ at Sunday Mass each week

❑ in the Sacrament of Reconciliation

I know these prayers by heart:

❑ Sign of the Cross

❑ Our Father

❑ Hail Mary

❑ Doxology (Glory to the Father)

❑ Morning Offering

❑ Act of Contrition

❑ Angel of God

I celebrate Jesus at Mass in these ways:

❑ listening to the readings and homily

❑ singing the songs

❑ making the responses

❑ offering Jesus and myself to the Father

❑ praying the Our Father

❑ reverently receiving Jesus in Holy Communion

I do these things to show Jesus love:

❑ respect my parents and others who care for me

❑ forgive those who hurt me

❑ share with others

❑ tell the truth when tempted to lie

❑ help those in need

❑ show care for other people and property

❑ pray and sacrifice for the poor, sick, lonely, and those who do not know Jesus

❑ **I can answer the questions on pages 132–134.**

God Gives Us Life and Love

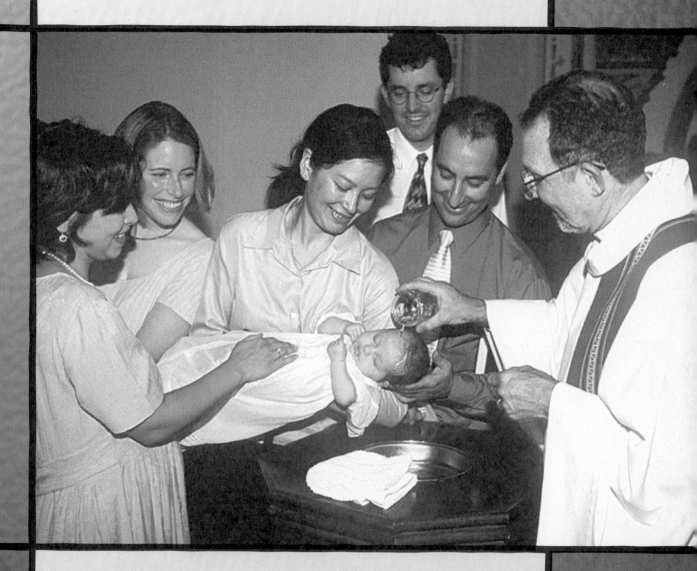

Our all-loving God gives us the gifts of life, love, and his Son, Jesus. Jesus calls us to intimacy with himself through his Church. In this first unit the children are led to a deeper awareness of God's presence in the love, beauty, and goodness of the gifts God gives them each day. They learn how they can open their hearts to the life God shared with them at Baptism.

God's Gifts Show God's Goodness and Love

God is the GIVER OF GIFTS.
God gives the gift of summer.
I feel the warm sun on my back
and cool blades of grass beneath my feet.
And I know that GOD IS GOOD!

God sends the gifts of rain, colorful flowers,
trees to climb, and lakes with waves.
I know the gift of the touch of a
soft, furry kitten and a puppy's lick on my face.
And I know that GOD IS GOOD!

God gives the gift of people who love me
and care when I fall and scrape my knee,
when I'm thirsty for lemonade, when I
feel sad and lonely and hungry for a hug.
And I know that GOD LOVES ME!

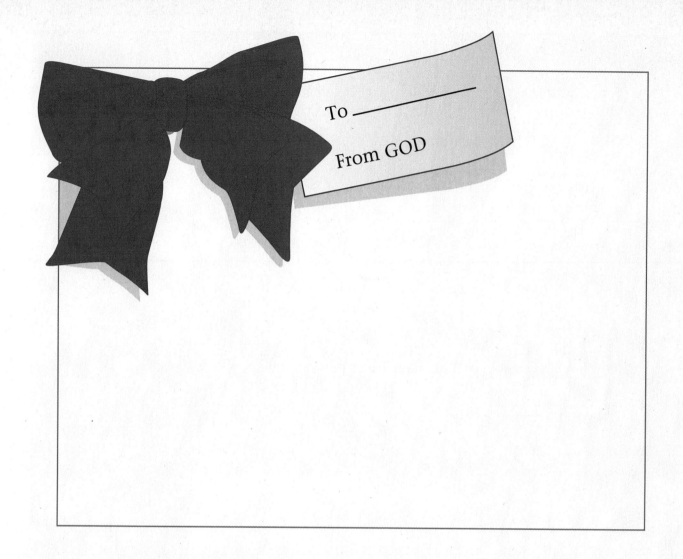

What gift of God is special to you and
your family?

Draw the gift in the gift box above. Print
your name on the tag.

Was it hard to choose just one gift?
God is good to give us so many gifts.
What would you like to say to God
when you think about God's gifts to you?

Print it here:

We Are Gifts

Everything God made is a gift. God
made us. We are gifts. God made us like
himself. We can think. We can choose.
We can love.

Gifts are to be given. We give ourselves
to others. We give ourselves to God.

I give you thanks for making me so wonderful.

adapted from Psalm 139:14

We have a mind so that we can **think.**

Print one thing you learned last year.

_____

- -

_____

We can **choose.**

Choose the pet you like best.
Make a circle around it.

God has given us a heart to **love** with.

Whom do you love in a special way?

Write their names or draw their pictures in the heart.

God Cares for His Gifts

One day Jesus said,

"God loves you more than the birds.
He loves you more than the flowers.
God takes good care of you."

adapted from Luke 12:24–29

Trace the bird and the flowers.
Color them.

How do you care for God's gifts?

Each Person Is a Special Gift

Put a check above each person God made and loves.

We Remember

How did God make us?
God made us in the image and likeness of himself. We can think, choose, and love.

We Respond

How wonderful are your gifts. They are more than I can count.

adapted from Psalm 40:6

FAMILY CORNER

All of creation speaks of God's love, beauty, and goodness; but the gift of human life sets people apart from other creatures. Every person is made in the image of God and is called to cooperate in caring for his gifts.

Read
Luke 12:24–29

Discuss
• a way in which you have experienced God's loving care
• how we can care for ourselves, other people, and God's world

Pray
Thank you, Lord, for all your gifts.

Do
• Have each family member decide on a special way to show love to someone.
• At meal prayer each day, thank God for a particular gift that someone noticed.
• Have someone print and decorate the psalm prayer in "We Respond." Post it on a mirror or on the refrigerator.
• Make your child aware that choices have consequences: We can't have red shoes if we choose brown ones.
• Read a story that evokes appreciation for nature: *Time of Wonder* by Robert McCloskey or *A Tree Is Nice* by Janice Udry.

❑ Signature

Jesus Shows Us the Father's Love

Amy was playing in the lake. A big wave knocked her down. Under the water Amy couldn't breathe. She couldn't cry out. She kicked and splashed. She thought she was going to die.

Then Amy felt someone's arms around her. She was lifted up into the air. She could see the sun again. Her big brother had saved her life.

The Father sent Jesus to save us. Jesus is God's best gift to us. He tells us about God. He teaches us how to live.

Most wonderful of all, Jesus gives us **new life.**

Jesus once told a story about a seed. He said,

> "It must die. If it dies, it brings forth much fruit."

adapted from John 12:23–24

Jesus died for our sins so that we could live forever. Jesus suffered and died on the cross. Then he rose from the dead with new life. He shares this new life with us. We can go to heaven. Jesus is our **Savior.**

ALLELUIA!

The Story of a Seed

Trace the dotted lines. Color the pictures.

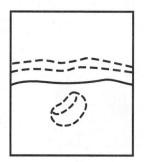

When you plant a seed, it dies.

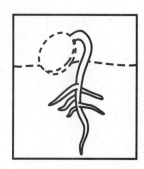

It grows into a new plant.

Flowers grow. Fruit grows.

We Remember That Jesus Saved Us

We remember Jesus' love.
We make the **Sign of the Cross.**

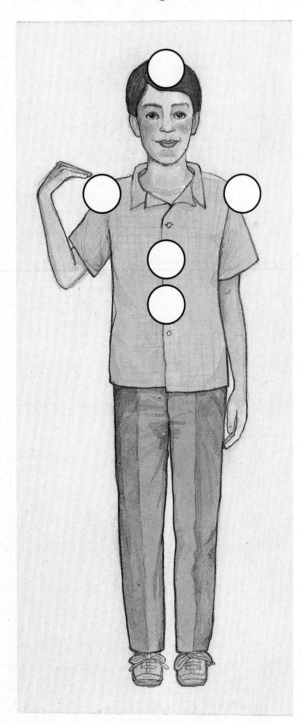

1. In the name of the Father,

2. and of the Son,

3. and of the Holy

4. Spirit.

5. Amen.

Where is your hand when you say these words?

Number the circles to match the words. To show how your hand moves, draw lines connecting the circles.

Friends of Jesus Are the Church

Jesus called people to be his friends. He called Peter, Andrew, James, and John from their boats. "Follow me," Jesus invited. These friends became his **disciples,** his **Church.**

Mary, the Mother of God, is the Mother of the Church. Everyone in the Church tries to live and love like Jesus. Jesus called you to be his friend.

You are a disciple. As a member of the Church, you share the life of Jesus. We call this life **grace.**

Jesus Shares His Life with Us

Jesus told us about our life with him.

He said,

> "I am the vine, you are the branches.
> You must live in me, as I live in you.
> A branch cannot bear fruit if it is cut
> off from the vine. If you live in me, you
> can do many good things."
>
> adapted from John 15:5–7

Color the vine and the branches to
make them more beautiful.

Trace over the words and read
the message.

Jesus is the vine. We are the branches.

Our good deeds are the fruit.

We Remember

How did Jesus show us the Father's love?
Jesus died and rose to bring us new life.

What did Jesus say about our life and his?
Jesus said,

"I am the vine, you are the branches."

John 15:5

We Respond

Thank you, God our Father, for your best gift, Jesus.

FAMILY CORNER

God shows his love for the human family by giving us his Son. Jesus died and rose to save us. He shows us how we can be happy every day. Because of Jesus we can live with God forever.

 Read
John 14:6–7

Discuss
- how it feels to be lost and how good it is to find the way again
- how we come to know God better by listening to Jesus' words

 Pray
Here I am, Lord! I come to do your will.

Do
- Take turns telling something you know about Jesus.
- Take a nature walk and see how life comes from death: flowers come from seeds.

❑ Signature

13

God Gives New Life in Baptism

At **Baptism** Jesus gave us grace, a share in his life. He took away all our sin. His Spirit came to live in us. We became God's children. We became members of God's family, the Church.

> Think of how God loves us. He calls us his children and that is what we are.
>
> adapted from 1 John 3:1

We received

FAITH

HOPE

LOVE

Baptism is a sacrament. A **sacrament** is a way that the Church meets Jesus. It is a special celebration of God's family.

We Belong to the Church

People who believe in Jesus are a community of love. They are called **Christians.** They try to worship and to love as Jesus did. They are God's people, the **Church.** You belong to the **Catholic Church,** a part of God's people.

You are no longer strangers or visitors. You belong to the saints and are part of God's people.

adapted from Ephesians 2:19

Add yourself to this picture of the Church.

The Church Welcomed Us in Baptism

Here are pictures of Tom Hunt's Baptism from the Hunt family photo album.

Father Bob greets Tom, saying, "The Christian family welcomes you with great joy." He and Tom's parents make the Sign of the Cross on Tom.

Father Bob reads from the Bible. Then he and the people pray, "Give this child the new life of Baptism."

The parents and **godparents** promise to help Tom live as a good Christian.

Father Bob baptizes Tom. He pours **water** and says, "Thomas, I baptize you in the name of the Father, and of the Son, and of the Holy Spirit."

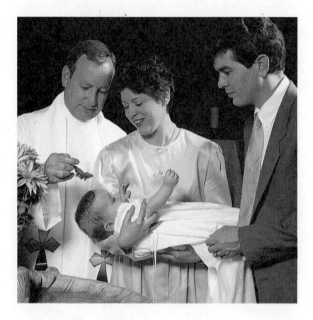

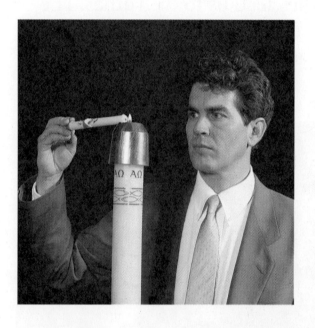

A **candle** is lighted. Father Bob says, "Receive the light of Christ."

The family and friends are filled with joy.

They celebrate Tom's new life.

Father Bob lays a **white robe** on Tom. He says, "You have clothed yourself in Christ."

Jesus Helps Us through His Church

The risen Jesus lives in the Church. He is the head of his Church. He sent the Holy Spirit to help us, who belong to the Church.

Jesus gave leaders to his Church. They help us grow in God's life. They lead us to the Father. The twelve **apostles** were the first leaders.

Color the shapes marked *.

You will see the names of the leaders of our Church today.

We help one another to build up the Church. We use the gifts God has given us.

18

_____

- -

_____

Print your name in the box. Use pretty colors to show that you are a Christian and have new life.

We Remember

What did Jesus give us when we were baptized?

Jesus gave us a share in his life.

What is a Christian?

A Christian is a person who believes in Jesus and tries to love as Jesus did. Many Christians belong to the Catholic Church.

Words to Know

Baptism	apostles
sacrament	pope
faith	bishops
hope	Christian
love	Catholic Church

We Respond

Father, help us share our gifts with others to build up the Church.

FAMILY CORNER

Baptism initiates us into the family of Christ and requires that we act in keeping with our new dignity. Christians are called to live in love, united with all the People of God under the leadership of the pope and bishops.

 Read
1 John 4:9–12

Discuss
- how sharing and giving are signs of love
- why you brought your child to be baptized
- ways you try to show you care about others as God does

 Pray
Dear Jesus, help me grow in love of you.

Do
- Put everyone's baptismal day on the family calendar.
- Decide on a way your family can show the light of God's love to others.
- Find out more about the baptismal patron of each family member.
- Make a family candle. Light it at family meals and prayer times.
- Post the prayer for this week on the bathroom mirror.

❏ Signature

19

Jesus Helps Us Hear God Speak

Jesus came to visit a little town. Some people brought a deaf man to him. The man could not hear or speak. The people asked Jesus to help him. Jesus touched the man's ears and mouth, and said, "Be opened." At once the man could hear and speak. All the people said, "Jesus has done good things."

adapted from Mark 7:31–37

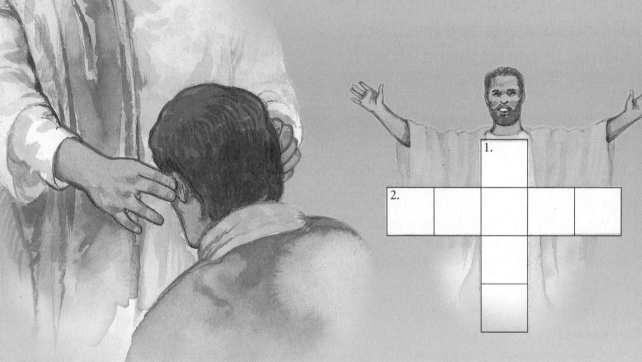

Read the clues for filling in the words of the puzzle. Find the words in the story and print them in the boxes.

1. The man can do this with his ears.

2. He can do this with his mouth.

Our Hearts Are Opened to God's Call

In Baptism God opened my heart to hear him. Now God speaks to me every day. God calls me to know him in everything that is. God speaks to me in the Bible.

God speaks to me through Jesus, who came to show us the Father's love. I can speak to others about God.

Church Puzzle

Words in candle: Mary, love, Jesus, life, Church, Savior, Baptism, Christian, bishops

Read the clues for the puzzles in the church window. Find the correct words in the candle and print them in the puzzles.

Draw a flame and some rays for the candle.

Top Puzzle
1. Another name for Jesus, the head of the Church
2. The Mother of the Church
3. A community that believes in Jesus

Left Puzzle
1. Leaders of the Church
2. _____ showed the Church how to live.
3. Christians try to _____ as Jesus did.

Right Puzzle
1. Someone who tries to live like Jesus
2. God shared his _____ with us at Baptism.
3. We became God's children at _____.

Christians Use Their Gifts for God

When John Bosco was a boy, he learned how to do many tricks. He could juggle and do other stunts.

John used his gifts, his tricks, to spread God's love. After his friends said their prayers or took part in Mass, he would do some tricks for them.

John became a priest when he grew up. He started a home and school for boys. John showed them how to love God and how to use their gifts for God.

God has given gifts to everyone. We can use our gifts to help people love God.

FAMILY CORNER

Belonging to a group gives the members both joys and responsibilities. The Church is a community of people who believe in Jesus and share his mission. God has given each person different gifts for the benefit of others.

 Read
1 Corinthians 12:12–20

Discuss
- the unique ways that each one in the family helps the others and needs the others
- examples of ways that one person's decisions and actions affect others

 Pray
Dear Jesus, help me share my love with someone today.

Do
- Ask your child to tell you the story of St. John Bosco.
- Decide on something you each would like to learn. Plan how to help one another do it.
- Before each evening meal mention ways others have helped you that day and thank the Lord.
- Read a story that tells how people made sacrifices for others: *The Hole in the Dike* retold by Norma Green or *The Bears on Hemlock Mountain* by Alice Dalgliesh.

_____

❑ Signature

Jesus Calls Us to Give Ourselves in Love

In this unit the children learn that Catholics show their love for God through daily prayer, reverence in speaking his name, and participation in Sunday Mass. They hear Jesus asking them to love others as he loves them, and they learn that love shows itself in obedience and in kind, pure, honest, and truthful words and deeds.

Jesus Loved God His Father

We like to celebrate. God made us to celebrate his love. He made us to love and be joyful.

Jesus said:

> "Live in my love. Keep my **commandments.** Then my joy will be in you, and your joy will be full."
>
> adapted from John 15:10–11

Jesus loved his Father very much. He always did what pleased his Father.

Jesus loved talking to him. He heard his Father speaking to him in everything.

Jesus spoke of his Father with love.

He celebrated the Lord's Day.

Jesus told us,

"Love the Lord your God with all your heart."

Mark 12:30

Christians celebrate God's love always and everywhere. Celebrating and loving God make us happy.

Catholics especially celebrate God's love together as the Church at Sunday Mass.

Print the missing words from the hearts.

God's law in the Bible tells how to love him. We show God love

_____
_____

when we _____,

_____
_____

say his _____ with love,

_____
_____

and celebrate the _____ .

pray

name

Lord's Day

Ask your mother or father to sign this page if you can pray the Our Father by heart.

_____

We Can Pray to God Every Day

LORD, you know me so well. You know
   everything I do.
You know when I sit and when I stand.
You read my thoughts from far away.
When I work and when I rest, you
   watch over me.
There is nothing I say that you do
   not know.
You are all around me, saving me with
   your hand.

adapted from Psalm 139:1–5

Color the picture. Make it beautiful.

Make word banners. Fill in the missing words by using the clues at the bottom of the page.

Across

1. We p _ _ _ when we talk and listen to God.
3. The Lord's Day is S _ _ _ _ _ _ .
6. When we keep God's commandments, we have j _ _ in our hearts.
7. We take part in M _ _ _ to celebrate the Lord's Day.

Down

2. Sunday is a day to r _ _ _ from hard work.
4. We honor God's n _ _ _ .
5. We l _ _ _ God with our whole heart.
8. We s _ _ _ and pray in church.

Work the puzzle. Use this code.

e	h	r	v	w	y
1	2	3	4	5	6

God is

1	4	1	3	6	5	2	1	3	1

Write the word that is missing from the sentences.

Our Father shows that he loves us. We show God that we love him when we pray.

_____

We _____ in the morning.

_____

We _____ during the day.

_____

We _____ at night.

We Remember

What is the greatest law?
The greatest law is "Love the Lord your God with all your heart and soul."

How do we live this law?
We live this law by praying, saying God's name with love, and celebrating the Lord's Day. We also try to do what God wants.

Words to Know
commandments   Lord's Day

We Respond

God, may I show my love by praying, saying your name with love, and celebrating your day.

FAMILY CORNER

God alone can give us true happiness. Jesus, responding to his Father in all things, shows us how everything, even suffering, can lead us to him. We show that we want to live in communion with God by praying, speaking of him with love, and celebrating the Eucharist on his day.

 Read
Ephesians 5:19–20

Discuss
- how you can pray more frequently together
- times when Jesus turned to his Father in prayer (Mark 1:35)
- which prayer each one likes best and why

 Pray
My God, I love you!

Do
- Plan a way to make Sunday special.
- Print the name JESUS on a card. Post it by a crucifix and explain why some people bow their heads when Jesus' name is said.
- Pray Psalm 139 on page 28 as part of your daily evening prayer.
- Check your child's understanding and memorization of the Our Father.

_____

❏ Signature

Jesus Gave Us a Law of Love

Jesus said,

"Love one another as I love you."

John 15:12

"Love your enemies."

Luke 6:27

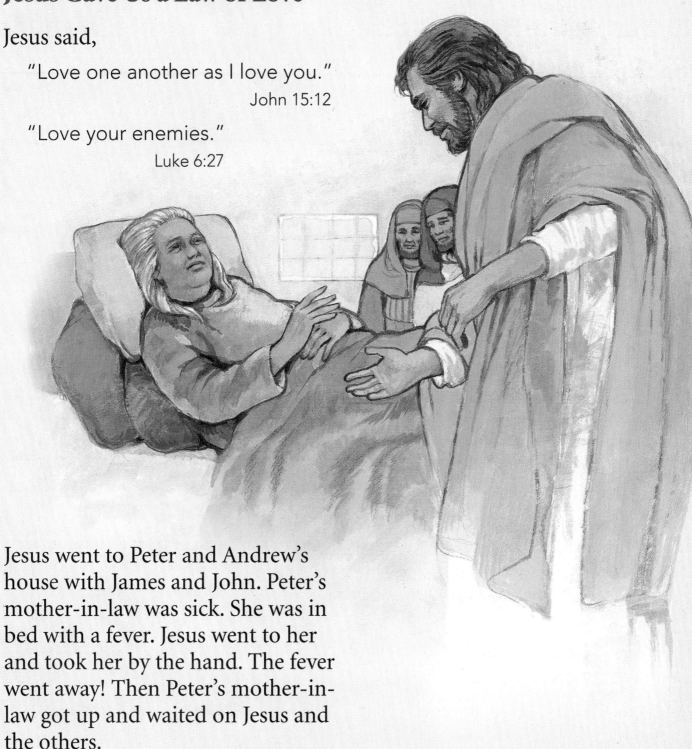

Jesus went to Peter and Andrew's house with James and John. Peter's mother-in-law was sick. She was in bed with a fever. Jesus went to her and took her by the hand. The fever went away! Then Peter's mother-in-law got up and waited on Jesus and the others.

Jesus followed God's law in the Bible.

This law shows us how to love others.

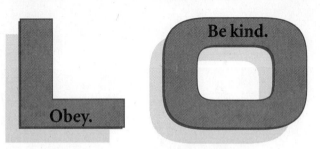

Obey. Be kind. Be pure. Be honest. Be truthful.

Match the pictures with the words of Jesus. Put the right number in the boxes.

I will remember Jesus' words:
1. I was thirsty and you gave me a drink.
2. I was hungry and you gave me food.
3. I was sick and you visited me.
4. I was a stranger and you made me welcome.

adapted from Matthew 25:35–36

32

We Obey When We Listen to God Our Father

Jesus said,

"I always do the things that please my Father."
adapted from John 14:31

Mary and Joseph took Jesus to the Temple. On the way home he was not with them. Jesus was lost. After three days Mary and Joseph found him in the Temple. He was talking to the teachers. He was doing his Father's work. Jesus went back with Mary and Joseph to Nazareth. He listened to his Father and obeyed Mary and Joseph.

We listen to God our Father when we **obey** those who take care of us.

Color the picture. See how beautiful you can make it look.

Ways to Obey

Complete the sentences under the pictures
with the words in the boxes.

| work | come | help | pray |

I will do things that please Jesus.

I will _____ others.

I will _____ to God.

I will _____ hard
at school.

I will _____ when
called.

What can you turn each day into?

Write the letter in the box that comes before each letter under it.

B	L	J	O	E	O	F	T	T		E	B	Z

Put a star in the box each time you are kind on that day.

Monday	Tuesday	Wednesday	Thursday	Friday	Saturday	Sunday

Word to Know

obey

We Remember

What is the new commandment of Jesus?

The new commandment of Jesus is "Love one another as I love you."

We Respond

Jesus, help me to be loving. Help me to obey those who take care of me.

FAMILY CORNER

Jesus tells us to love others as he loves us. We love as Jesus does when we are kind, helpful, thoughtful, and obedient. Jesus tells us that whatever we do to others we do to him.

 Read
Matthew 25:35–40

Discuss
- how your family can support parish and community efforts to help those in need
- what you as a family can do to show you really care for each other

 Pray
All for you, O Lord!

Do
- Read or tell of incidents that show how the saints used their gifts to help others.
- Make a sign that says, "Whatever you do to others you do to me." Post it by a picture of Jesus or by the crucifix.
- Pray for people whose needs are broadcast in the day's news.
- Each evening answer the question, "Did we pass by anyone in need today?" Relate it particularly to unspoken needs. State what you could have done for another family member and apologize for not doing it. Each apology should be accepted with "That's OK" or some other sign of love.

❏ Signature

We Love When We Show Respect

Everything God made is good.
Everything is a gift of love from God.
We treat God's gifts carefully. We use
them as God meant them to be used.
We show we are grateful for them.

Write in the missing words.

Life is a special gift.

_____
_ _ _ _ _ _ _ _ _

We _____ all living things.
        respect

_____
_ _ _ _ _ _ _ _ _

We take _____ of them and help them grow.
        care

Every person is a gift from God. Everyone is loved by God as his child. Everyone is precious. You are precious, too. We show love and respect for persons when we are polite and

We show respect for ourselves and others when we respect our bodies and are

When we respect ourselves and others, we love God, who made us.
We live in God's love.
We are full of joy.

We Love When We Are Honest

God gave all of us earth's gifts. God wants us to share them and to be honest. We are honest when we respect other people's things. We do not take them. We are careful when we use them. We show God and others that we love them. This girl is returning a book. She is being

honest

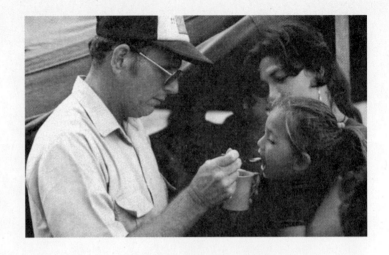

We Love When We Are Truthful

God loves what is true.
We all love the truth.
We love God and others when we tell the truth.
This girl is telling her mother that she broke a vase. She is being

truthful

Print on each balloon a word from the hearts that shows you respect life.

I am _____

I am _____

I am _____

I am _____

Draw one thing you can care for.

We Remember

What did Jesus say about anyone who loves?
Jesus said,

"God is love, and whoever remains in love remains in God and God in him."

1 John 4:16

We Respond

Dear Jesus, help me
✠ to respect your gifts and take care of them
✠ to be kind and pure
✠ to be honest and truthful.

Words to Know
kind honest pure truthful

FAMILY CORNER

We follow Christ's way of love when we are respectful, honest, and truthful. Jesus helps us see what is good and true when we pray.

Read
Romans 12:9–21

Discuss
• how we all are weak and make mistakes
• ways your family could better the lives of victims of an injustice in your community

Pray
I thank you, Lord, with all my heart.

Do
• Praise your child when he or she is kind, helpful, honest, or truthful. Children need encouragement to continue their efforts to reach out to others in love.
• Make a card and send it to a sick or an elderly person or a shut-in.
• Every day reassure your child that you love him or her. The habit of saying, "Good night, and I love you," makes it easier for a child to express love verbally.

❏ Signature

St. Thérèse Made Sacrifices for Others

Thérèse was a little girl who loved God very much. She gave the gift of herself to Jesus. Jesus gave himself to her in Holy Communion.

Every day Thérèse did the things that pleased God. She made **sacrifices** for people who didn't know God.

Thérèse asked Jesus to help her and all people to love him more.

St. Thérèse,
Little Flower of Jesus,
pray for us.

Color a petal on the rose each time you make a sacrifice to God.

God Calls Us to Give Ourselves

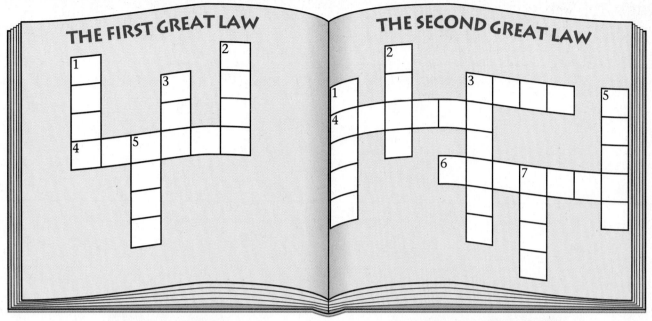

THE FIRST GREAT LAW

THE SECOND GREAT LAW

LOVE GOD

LOVE OTHERS

Read the clues. Print the answers in the puzzles above.

name	obey	God	share
Mass	respect	Sunday	kind
pray	honest	truth	others
pure			

Across

4. Christians celebrate God's day on ____.

Down

1. Catholics celebrate God's day by taking part in ____.
2. We talk to God when we ____.
3. The first great law tells us to love ____.
5. When we pray, we use God's holy ____.

Across

3. When we do what God wants, we ____.
4. When we take only things that belong to us, we are ____.
6. When we are polite to others, we show ____.

Down

1. When we give to others, we ____.
2. When we help others, we are ____.
3. God's second great law tells us to love ____.
5. When we say what really happened, we tell the ____.
7. When we respect our bodies and the bodies of others, we are ____.

Connect the dots to finish this picture. You will see who you are like when you love God and love others.

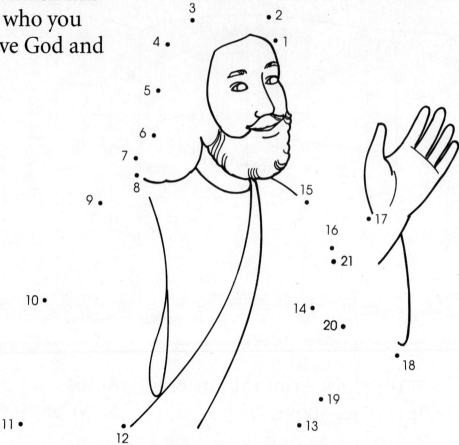

FAMILY CORNER

Keeping God's law and loving God and others may mean making sacrifices. We gladly give ourselves to God and our brothers and sisters just as Jesus did.

Read
John 15:11–17

Discuss
- ways each family member helps the others
- sacrifices involved in loving

Pray
Think of one or two people who need help and pray: Bless them, Lord.

Do
- Read a story that shows how insensitivity to others' needs makes people sad: *The Hundred Dresses* by Eleanor Estes.
- Do something that will help a new family in the parish or neighborhood feel welcome.
- Point out during a television program how someone is keeping or not keeping God's law of love. Discuss it afterwards.

_____

❏ Signature

God's Ten Laws of Love

The Eisenbergs are a Jewish family. Thirteen-year-old Aaron has just celebrated his Bar Mitzvah. This means "son of the commandment." Aaron's Bar Mitzvah marks his willingness to live by the law of God.

Jewish people treasure God's laws. In their synagogues and temples, the books of the Bible that contain the law or Commandments are kept in an ark, or cabinet. This ark has a place of honor and a light burning before it just as the tabernacles in our churches have.

In Scripture, after giving Moses the Ten Commandments, God said, "Take to heart these words. . . . Drill them into your children. . . . Bind them at your wrists as a sign and let them be as a pendant on your forehead. Write them on the doorposts of your houses" (Deuteronomy 6:6–9).

From the time of his Bar Mitzvah, whenever Aaron prays he may wear phylacteries just as his father and other Jewish men do. These are boxes that contain Deuteronomy 6:4–9 and other Scripture passages. They are tied with leather straps to the left arm and to the forehead.

On the front doorpost of the Eisenberg home is a small box called a mezuzah, which means "doorpost." In it too is a parchment with words of God from Deuteronomy. The mezuzah reminds the Eisenbergs of God's law and lets everyone know they are a Jewish family.

Although sometimes Christian girls wear bracelets that have the Ten Commandments on them, our zeal for God's law is not often publicly displayed. More important than displaying the Commandments is *living* according to them.

Celebrating God's Law

Because your child has just studied the Ten Commandments, your family might plan a day to celebrate God's law, incorporating some of the following ideas:

1. Enjoy making and eating tablet-shaped cookies.

2. As a family project, shape dough to form two tablets. With a toothpick carve into them the Roman numerals from one through ten. Allow the tablets to harden, or bake them. Paint them and spray them with acrylic. Then display the tablets in your home.

3. Pray together parts of Psalm 119, which is a hymn praising God's law.

4. Watch the video *The Ten Commandments*.

5. Make a Law of Love tree as a centerpiece for your table. Use branches or two wire hangers stretched out. Set these in Styrofoam or plaster of paris. Print key words for the commandments on pink paper hearts and tie the hearts to the tree: *Pray, God's Name, God's Day, Obey, Pure, Kind, Truthful,* and *Honest*.

6. Have one person hide the key words for the commandments. After the other family members have found them, arrange them in order.

7. Put on skits that show someone keeping one of the commandments.

Guides to God

As we follow God's Ten Commandments we try to be perfect-10 human beings. Go through the maze to reach Jesus. Talk about each commandment as its sign is passed.

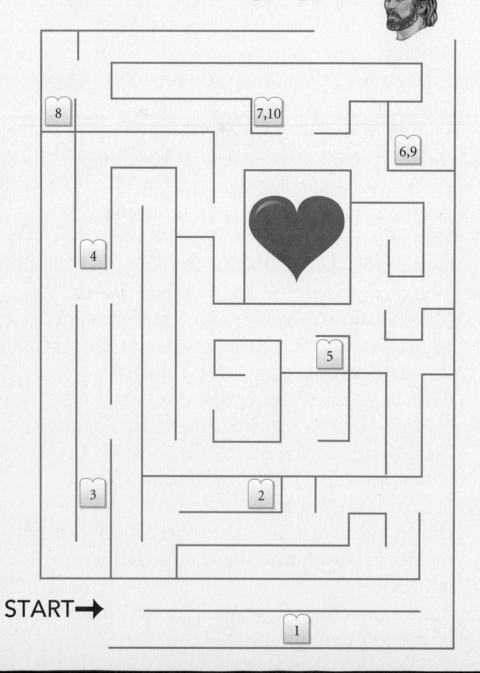

Jesus Gives Us the Gift of Peace

The Gospel stories show us God's great love for sinners. Jesus extends this same forgiving love to us in the Sacrament of Reconciliation (Penance). Each chapter in this unit prepares the children for their first celebration of the sacrament by leading them to a deeper relationship with the Lord and to reconciliation with him when they have failed to love.

Jesus Chose Us to Be His Friends

We choose our friends. Friends are happy together. They share with one another.

Jesus chose us to be his friends. He wants to share his life and love with us. Jesus wants to share his heavenly home, too. He said,

> "You are my friends if you do what I command you."
>
> John 15:14

Jesus tells us to love God our Father. He tells us to love others.

Jesus Is Always Our Friend

Jesus always loves us, but we do not always love our friends.

Sometimes we are selfish.

Then we are not good friends.

We say we are sorry.

Then we become friends again.

Sometimes we are not good friends of Jesus. We choose to do things he does not like. We fail to love God our Father. We fail to love others.

We tell Jesus we are sorry.

Jesus Forgave Zacchaeus

Use the pictures to tell the story of Zacchaeus. Luke 19:1–10

Jesus forgave Zacchaeus when he was sorry. Jesus forgives us when we are sorry. He shares his peace and joy with us. We try to be better friends of Jesus by being more loving.

Second graders wrote these notes.

Dear Sam,

I'm sorry I hurt your feelings. Please forgive me. This summer I will invite you to my party. I will not hurt you anymore. I'm sorry.

Love,
Mark

Dear Greg,

I am sorry for the bad words that I called you. I really never meant them.

Love,
Jimmy

Write an "I'm sorry" note to Jesus.

_____

_ _

_____

We Remember

When are we friends of Jesus?

Jesus said,

"You are my friends if you do what I command you."

John 15:14

We Respond

Jesus, I want to be your good friend. Be with me to help me love God my Father and other people.

FAMILY CORNER

No matter what we do, Jesus is always ready to be our friend. Through Jesus we see that God calls sinners to receive his forgiveness and peace. Jesus invites us, as he welcomed Zacchaeus, to a change of heart.

Read
Luke 19:1–10

Discuss

• how Jesus showed he loved Zacchaeus
• how we know Jesus loves us
• how we can welcome Jesus into our hearts and homes
• ways we can ask and show forgiveness

Pray
O my God, help me to love you and others more.

Do

• Ask your child to tell you about pages 2 and 3 in the Reconciliation Booklet. Help him or her find a photo or draw a portrait for page 2. Ask your child to tell you one of the stories on pages 4, 5, and 6.
• Help your child express sorrow each evening for selfish, thoughtless, or hurtful words and actions. Your child may conclude by telling Jesus how he or she will try to be a better friend.
• Pray with your child an "I'm Sorry" prayer. One form is on the back inside cover of this book.
• Read *Rotten Ralph* by Jack Gantos.

_____

❏ Signature

We Are Happy When We Say Yes to God

God tells us how to be happy. He said, "Love God and others." When we love God and others, we say yes to God.

We Need Jesus' Forgiveness

When we choose to be selfish and fail to love God and others, we say no to God.

We commit a **sin.** We need **forgiveness** from God and his family.

Print a **Y** in the box if the picture shows children saying yes to God.

Circle what sin is:

a temptation

saying no to God

an accident

an unloving act

a mistake

Jesus Gives Us a Sacrament of Peace

Fill in the missing words. The words on the Easter basket will help you. You may use them more than once. Color the basket and draw eggs in it. Eggs stand for new life.

_____

On the evening of the first _____
Sunday, Jesus went to see the apostles.

"_____

He said to them, _____ be with you."

_____

The apostles were filled with joy to see _____.

Jesus said: "Receive the Holy Spirit.
Whose sins you forgive are forgiven them."

adapted from John 20:19–23

Jesus gave us the **Sacrament of Reconciliation.**

_____

It was his Easter _____ to us.

_____

It was his gift to bring us _____.

gift   Easter
Jesus   peace

Jesus Forgave the Woman Who Had Sinned

A woman who had sinned came to Jesus.
She was sorry for her sins and began to
cry. Jesus looked at her with love.

Simon and the other people at the table
were not pleased. They thought Jesus
should not let a sinner touch him. Jesus
said to them, "She has loved more than
you. Her sins have been forgiven."

Then Jesus told the woman, "Your sins
are forgiven. Go in peace."

adapted from Luke 7:36–50

She would try to be a good friend of
Jesus. She knew Jesus would help her.

Write Yes or No on the lines.

1. Do we love God when we fail to keep his laws? _____
2. Do we love God when we tell him we are sorry? _____
3. Does Jesus forgive us when we are sorry? _____
4. Do we have peace after Jesus forgives us? _____
5. Did Jesus give his apostles power to forgive sins? _____
6. Is a temptation a sin? _____
7. Did Jesus give us the Sacrament of Baptism
   on Easter Sunday? _____

We Remember

What is sin?

Sin is choosing to say no to God. Sin offends God and hurts others and ourselves.

When does Jesus forgive our sins?

Jesus forgives our sins when we are sorry.

Words to Know

sin   temptation   peace
Sacrament of Reconciliation

We Respond

O my God, I am very sorry for all my sins because they displease you, who are all good and deserving of all my love. With your help I will sin no more. Amen.

FAMILY CORNER

Jesus continually calls us who have sinned to reconciliation. In the Sacrament of Penance he gives us a sign of his divine forgiveness and leads us to greater peace.

 Read
John 20:19–23

Discuss
- how the priest talks to us in the Sacrament of Reconciliation, helps us know what we can do to be more loving, forgives us in Jesus' name, and brings us God's peace
- how people can experience the peace of being reconciled and become more loving

 Pray
Lord, have mercy.

Do
- Help your child print his or her own "I'm Sorry" prayer on page 9 of the Reconciliation Booklet.
- Talk about times you needed to be forgiven and how you showed more love.
- Show your child the reconciliation room or the confessional in your church.

_____
❏ Signature

The Spirit of Jesus Is with Us

Jesus said,

> "I will send my Spirit to be with you always."
>
> adapted from John 14:16

We received the Spirit of Jesus when we were baptized. His Spirit helps us to love God and one another.

Love, peace, and joy are signs of the **Holy Spirit.**

We love God when we love one another.

We are to pray for other people.

We are to be kind and fair to everyone. We are to help our parents and obey them.

God the Holy Spirit is within us. The Spirit helps us share his love, peace, and joy with others.

Write a prayer to the Holy Spirit.

_____

_____

_____

_____

_____

The Holy Spirit Helps Us Look into Our Hearts

We ask the Holy Spirit to help us look into our hearts. We ask the Spirit to help us know how we have loved God and others.

We thank Jesus for the loving things he helped us do. We tell Jesus we are sorry for the unloving things we did. Then Jesus forgives us. He gives us his love, peace, and joy. We are happy.

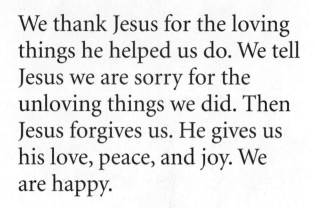

We ask ourselves two big questions. Can you finish them?

How have I loved _____ ?

How have I loved _____ ?

Each Day We Can Look into Our Hearts

Find the unloving words in the heart. Put an **X** on them.

truthful   respect

fight   love   lies

care   obey

help

honest   selfish

mean words

share

What does the Holy Spirit do for us?

The Holy Spirit helps us to love God and one another. The Spirit helps us look into our hearts.

> ### Words to Know
> Holy Spirit

We Respond

Come, Holy Spirit, fill my heart with your love.

FAMILY CORNER

The Spirit of Jesus is with us always and helps us see ourselves as we are before God. With the help of the Spirit we become aware of how we love God and others. When we listen to the Holy Spirit, our lives and actions can be filled with love, peace, and joy.

Read
John 14:23–27

Discuss
• the importance of taking time each day to listen to the Holy Spirit
• how we know when the Holy Spirit is asking us to do something good

Pray
Come, Holy Spirit, fill our hearts with your love.

Do
• Share with your child a time you changed because you listened to the Holy Spirit.
• Help your child form the habit of looking into his or her heart each day to recognize acts of love or failures to show love. Pages 10–14 of the Reconciliation Booklet can help you.
• When your child quarrels with or is mean to a brother, sister, or friend, reflect together on the reasons for the quarrel or meanness and discuss ways to handle the situation.

❏ Signature

We Like Being with People We Love

We like going to see people we love.
They always make us feel happy.

Here are the names of some people
I like to be with:

_____

_____

_____

_____

_____

_____

Jesus Forgives Us in the Sacrament of Peace

Children met Jesus when he lived on earth. Jesus loved them and blessed them.

We meet Jesus in the Sacrament of Reconciliation. We meet him in the priest who acts in Jesus' place. Jesus blesses and forgives us through the priest.

Print each word from the rainbow where it belongs in a sentence.

rainbow words: penance · peace · priest · pray · pardons

1. I _____ to the Holy Spirit.

2. I confess my sins to the _____ _____ .

3. The priest gives a _____ _____ .

4. The priest _____ _____ me in Jesus' name.

5. I go in _____ _____ .

We Remember

Who forgives our sins in the Sacrament of Reconciliation?
Jesus forgives our sins in the Sacrament of Reconciliation.

Words to Know

confess   penance   pardon

We Respond

Jesus, I'm sorry for my sins.

FAMILY CORNER

In the Sacrament of Reconciliation (Penance), God's forgiving love reaches out to us through the ministry of the Church. God pardons us whenever we confess our sins and express our desire to be more faithful to the teachings and example of Jesus.

Read
Matthew 5:23–24

Discuss
- how we change sad and heavy hearts when we accept signs of love from those who ask forgiveness
- how our smiles and our concern for others are better gifts than those money can buy

Pray
Thank the Lord, for he is good! His mercy endures forever!

Do
- Gently ask your child how he or she hurts others and offends God. See pages 10–14 in the Reconciliation Booklet.
- Encourage your child to apologize. Set an example by saying you are sorry when you do something wrong that affects your child.
- Discuss page 15 in the Reconciliation Booklet. Demonstrate how to greet the priest, how to express sorrow, and how to make up by doing a penance.

❑ Signature _____

God Forgives and
Helps Us to Be Better

Once King David did something that displeased God, but he made up for his sin. He told God he was sorry. David said:

Forgive me, O God, in your goodness.
I have sinned against you. I have
    done what is wrong.
Take away all my sins. Put a new
    heart in me.
Fill me with joy and gladness. Make
    me willing to obey you.

adapted from Psalm 51:1–14

God forgave David and helped him to be a better person. Then David praised and thanked God.

In the Sacrament of Reconciliation, the priest helps us to do what David did. He tells us how to make up for being unloving. He tells us how to be more like Jesus.

We listen to the priest. We tell God we are sorry, and God forgives us. We praise and thank God for his goodness. We try to be better persons.

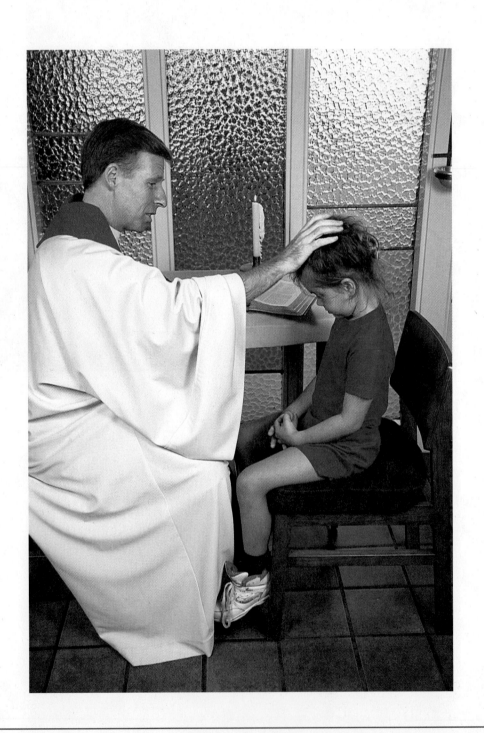

WE PRAISE GOD

My Praise Prayer

_____

_____

_____

_____

_____

_____

_____

_____

_____

Draw a line from the word (in the car) to its meaning (in the garage).

We Remember

What does Jesus do for us in the Sacrament of Reconciliation? Jesus forgives us, gives us his peace, and helps us to become better persons.

What is the most important thing for us to do in the Sacrament of Reconciliation? The most important thing for us to do is to be sorry for our sins.

How do we make up for our sins? We do penance, which may be prayers or good deeds.

We Respond

Give thanks to the LORD for he is good. His mercy endures forever.

adapted from Psalm 118:1

FAMILY CORNER

Our good God forgives us over and over. Each time we experience the wonder of his mercy, we respond with thanks and praise.

Read
Psalm 51:1–14

Discuss
• ways to make up for sin
• God's goodness in offering us mercy

Pray
Jesus, I love you!

Do
• Help your child memorize an act of contrition.
• Review pages 16–20 in the Reconciliation Booklet with your child.

❑ Signature

14

We Are Friends of Jesus

Mary and Martha were friends of Jesus. Mary listened to Jesus tell about his Father's love. Martha was kind to Jesus. She got food ready for him.

We are friends of Jesus, too. He wants us to listen to him as Mary did. He wants to tell us about his Father's love. He wants us to be kind like Martha. He wants us to share his Father's love.

Match the names with the pictures.
Put the number in the box.

1. The Lost Sheep
2. A Sinful Woman
3. Apostles
4. Jesus
5. The Sacrament of Peace
6. Zacchaeus

How Well Do You Remember?

Draw lines to match the two parts of these sentences.

The Holy Spirit helps us   •   •   the priest gives us.

We are sorry and want
to make up for   •   •   look into our hearts.

We do the penance that   •   •   our sins.

The penance may be   •   •   forgiveness and peace.

We praise and thank
Jesus for his   •   •   prayers or good deeds.

Write Yes or **No** on the lines.

1. Does Jesus love us even when we sin? _____

2. Does the priest forgive us in Jesus' name? _____

3. Does Jesus forgive us when we aren't sorry? _____

4. Do we sin **before** we have chosen to do wrong? _____

5. Do we meet Jesus when we celebrate the
   Sacrament of Reconciliation? _____

6. Are accidents sins? _____

7. Does Jesus forgive our sins in the Sacrament
   of Reconciliation? _____

8. Do our sins hurt God's family? _____

9. Do we love God when we fail to keep his laws? _____

10. Does Jesus help us to love God and others
    through the Sacrament of Reconciliation? _____

Meeting Jesus in the Sacrament of Reconciliation

Steps to Remember

1. Make the Sign of the Cross. Tell how long it has been since your last confession. Listen to the prayer the priest says, asking God to help you. Listen to him if he reads from the Bible.

2. Tell the priest your sins.

3. Listen to what the priest says and the penance he gives you.

4. Pray an Act of Contrition.

5. Make the Sign of the Cross silently when the priest gives you absolution.

6. When the priest says, "Give thanks to the Lord, for he is good," answer, "His mercy endures forever."

7. Thank the priest and leave.

Be sure to do the penance the priest gave you.

Print in each box the number of the step that goes with the word.

☐ confession ☐ sorrow

☐ a help to make up for sins ☐ pardon

FAMILY FEATURE

Peace in Our Homes

The Phans go as a family to celebrate the Sacrament of Reconciliation at their church. On the evening before, they meet together, and the family members ask pardon of one another for the times they failed to love. They read a story or passage from the Bible about sorrow for sin and God's loving mercy.

Mr. and Mrs. Phan bless their children. Then everyone prays the Our Father holding hands. Sometimes they sing a song such as "Peace Is Flowing like a River."

On the day of the sacrament, the Phans hang a paper dove in the dining room as a reminder of the renewed peace they experience from forgiveness. After receiving the sacrament, the family celebrates by going to an ice-cream parlor or a pizza restaurant.

When your child receives the Sacrament of Peace for the first time, you might wish to begin the tradition of a family reconciliation prayer service.

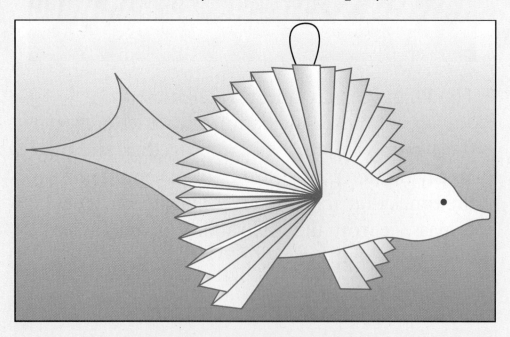

How to Make a Dove

1. Outline a dove on heavy white paper and cut it out.

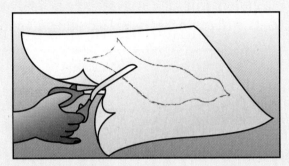

2. Make a slit in the side. Accordion-pleat a sheet of thin white paper.

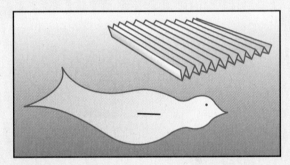

3. Insert the paper into the slit to make wings. To hang, tape wings together and thread string through them.

Mistakes and Sins

The world is not right when people sin. Sin destroys harmony and peace. How many things can your family find wrong in this picture?

KEEP OFF GRASS

A Family Reconciliation Celebration

(Have a crucifix available.)

Child: *(Lights a candle)*

Parent: Jesus says:

You are the light of the world. A city set on a mountain cannot be hidden. Nor do they light a lamp and then put it under a bushel basket; it is set on a lampstand, where it gives light to all in the house. Just so, your light must shine before others, that they may see your good deeds and glorify your heavenly Father.

Matthew 5:14–16

Parent: One of the best things about being a family is that we always belong. Even when we hurt somebody else in the family, we still belong. But when we hurt somebody in our family, we feel unhappy and our family is not together as it should be. So tonight we pray together and tell each other that we will try to be more loving and more forgiving.

All: *(Join hands and pray the Our Father.)*

Family: *(Everyone takes a turn to tell something the others do that makes him or her happy.)*

Parent: In the Sacrament of Reconciliation, God our Father brings us closer together with all the members of our family. Jesus tells us how we can be reconciled to one another. In a few days, [name of child] will celebrate the Sacrament of Reconciliation for the first time. In the sacrament, we tell the priest how we have failed to love and how we want to change our hearts as Zacchaeus did. Let us pray that we will be more loving after we meet Jesus in the Sacrament of Reconciliation.

Family: Stay with us, Lord, and be our joy!

Jesus Gives Us the Gift of Himself

Jesus so loves us that he gives himself to us in the Holy Eucharist. Each chapter in this unit increases the children's awareness of the Father's love and helps them participate meaningfully in the celebration of the Eucharist.

Jesus Is the Bread of Life

Jesus said,

"I am the bread of life; whoever comes to me will never hunger."

John 6:35

Mary Lou Skirbunt

The bread we re-ceive is the Bread of Life, al-le-lu- ia. Al-le-lu- ia.

Jesus Fed the People

A big crowd of people followed Jesus. They stayed with him all day. Jesus knew they were hungry at the end of the day. He wanted to feed them.

A boy in the crowd had five loaves of bread and two fish. Jesus took them and gave thanks to God our Father. Then he shared the bread and fish with all the people. They had as much as they wanted to eat. Twelve baskets of food were left over. Jesus had worked a **miracle.**

Jesus Promised to Give Living Bread

The next day the people found Jesus. He knew they had come because he had given them bread to eat.

He said to them, "You should work for bread that will help you live forever."

The people said, "Sir, give us this bread always."

Then Jesus promised the gift of the Holy Eucharist. He said,

"I am the living bread that came down from heaven; whoever eats this bread will live forever."

John 6:51

Many people did not believe Jesus. They asked, "How can he give us his Body and Blood to eat and drink?"

But the twelve apostles had faith. Peter said, "We believe."

Today Jesus comes to us in the forms of bread and wine.

Jesus is our food and drink

I believe.

Copy the words on the line. Draw crosses on the hosts. Draw red wine in the chalice. Color the picture.

Jesus Promised to Give Living Bread

Finish the sentences. Use the words in the bread.

The Holy Eucharist is _____ .

The sacred bread is his _____ .

The sacred wine is his _____ .

If we receive the Eucharist, we will live _____ .

We believe that Jesus can work this _____ .

(words in the bread: Jesus, forever, Body, miracle, Blood)

We Remember

What is the Eucharist?
The Eucharist is the sacrament in which we receive Jesus.

We Respond

Lord, you have the words of eternal life. I believe.

FAMILY CORNER

The food and drink of the Eucharist is Jesus. He is the Living Bread that gives us God's life and love, Bread that is broken and shared for the world's salvation.

Read
John 6:51–58

Discuss
• how sharing the Eucharist shows we believe what Jesus says and we want to obey God
• the significance of Jesus' giving himself in the form of food and drink to be shared
• how having friends over for a meal relates to the Eucharist: You share what you have. They deepen their friendship with you.

Pray
How good God is!

Do
• Talk about why we come together for Sunday Mass: to worship and thank our Father with, through, and in Jesus.
• Bake bread with your child (ready-to-bake mixes or frozen loaves). Share the bread after you read John 6:51, pray the Our Father, and discuss how bread is life-giving.

❏ Signature

God's People Celebrate Passover

Read each sentence and find the picture that shows it. Put the number of the sentence in the box. Tell the story to someone.

1. God freed his people.
2. God's people were slaves.
3. God's people celebrated a meal.
4. The blood of a lamb saved God's people from death.

Give thanks to the LORD, who is good.

Psalm 118:1

Jewish people still celebrate the **Passover** today.

Jesus Celebrates a Special Meal

On the night before Jesus died, he celebrated a special supper with his apostles. Before supper Jesus got a basin of water and a towel. He began to wash the feet of each apostle. When he finished, Jesus said,

> "If I, your master and teacher, have washed your feet, you should do things like this for one another."
>
> adapted from John 13:14–15

After that he gave us a new commandment:

> "As I have loved you, so you also should love one another."
>
> John 13:34

Jesus Gave the Gift of Himself at the Last Supper

At the **Last Supper,** Jesus took bread.
He thanked and praised his Father.
Then he blessed the bread and broke it.
He gave it to the apostles and said,

> "Take this, all of you, and eat it. This is
> **my Body,** which will be given up for you."

Then Jesus took the cup and blessed it.
He shared the wine with them, saying,

> "Take this, all of you, and drink from it.
> This is the cup of **my Blood.** It will be
> shed for you and for all so that sins
> may be forgiven."

Then Jesus said,

> "Do this in memory of me."
>> adapted from Luke 22:14–20

At the Last Supper, Jesus offered the gift
of himself to his Father. When he did
this, he gave us the **Mass.**

Come, Lord Jesus.

At Mass Jesus Gives Himself to the Father

Jesus loves his Father and us with the greatest love. Jesus gave himself to the Father as a sacrifice on the cross. A **sacrifice** is a gift given to God. Jesus gave up his life so that we could live with God forever.

The Mass is a gift that helps us remember and celebrate God's love.

At Mass, God speaks words of love to us. We listen to God's words. They tell us how we can give him gifts of love.

At Mass, Jesus offers himself to his Father for us. We offer the sacrifice of Jesus. We offer ourselves.

We can make everything we do a gift of love to God.

We Give Ourselves with Jesus

Puzzle Tree

Read the clues. Use the words in the flower patch to fill in the puzzle.

sign
Mass   pray
Supper   celebrate
wine   Body
Jesus

Down

1. Our work and play can be offered as a sacrifice at _____.
2. When we _____ the Mass, we offer the best sacrifice.
4. Every gift is a _____ of love.
6. We _____ with Jesus at Mass.

Across

3. _____ gave the best gift to God.
5. Jesus gave us the Eucharist at the Last _____.
7. At Mass, bread becomes Jesus' _____.
8. At Mass, the _____ becomes Jesus' Blood.

Morning Offering

God our Father, I offer you today
All I think and do and say.
I offer it with what was done
On earth by Jesus Christ, your Son.

Amen.

Tell how these children can make what they are doing a sacrifice.

We Remember

Who is sacrificed at Mass?
At Mass, Jesus gives himself to his Father for us. We offer Jesus and ourselves.

Why does Jesus come to us in Holy Communion?
Jesus comes to help us love God and others.

We Respond

Jesus, help me to prepare for my First Holy Communion by loving others as you love me.

Words to Know

Passover	sacrifice
Last Supper	Mass

FAMILY CORNER

The baptized are called to live united with Christ and his Church. At the Last Supper, Jesus gave the Church the means to join in the sacrifice of himself to the Father. At Mass, we unite ourselves with Jesus. We receive the Bread of Life in order to live in Christ and be united with God and one another.

Read
Luke 22:14–20

Discuss
- what you can offer with Jesus at every Mass
- how your words and actions at Mass show you love God
- what you as a family can do to participate more fully in the Mass

 Pray
Give thanks to the Lord, for he is good!

Do
- Teach your child the Grace Before Meals inside the back cover of this book.
- At supper share a thought, a word, or an act of the day that you offered to God.
- Ask your child to tell you about the Passover meal. Talk about how God asks us to remember Jesus' death and resurrection at Mass.
- Read a story that brings out the joy of self-sacrificing love.

❏ Signature

We Come with Love and Joy

Jesus invites God's people to the Eucharist.

At the Last Supper he said,

"Do this in memory of me."

Luke 22:19

"Friends, all gather 'round the table of the Lord."

Jesus wants his people to celebrate his victory over sin and death. He wants his people to praise and love the Father with him. Jesus wants children to come to his celebration, too. He told his friends,

"Let the children come to me."

Luke 18:16

The family of Jesus comes together to celebrate. We come to Mass to remember Jesus' dying and rising. We celebrate his great love and the love of our Father.

We begin when the priest and others walk to the altar. We praise God by singing together as his people.

These children are at Mass to celebrate.

Make the faces of the children show how happy they are. Draw yourself in the middle.

We Ask for Mercy

Jesus makes us all one in God's family. We come together to share the Eucharist, the meal of love.

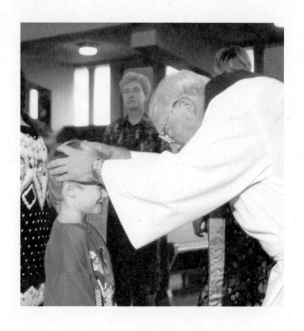

But sometimes we have not been loving. We have brought unhappiness to God's family.

We pray:
I confess to almighty God and to you, my brothers and sisters, that I have sinned through my own fault.

Then we ask God to forgive us:

Lord, have mercy.
Christ, have mercy.

_____

– – – – – – – – – – – – – – – – –

_____

Lord, have mercy.

Copy the words on the line.

The priest asks God to have mercy on us. God forgives us and we forgive one another. We are ready to celebrate.

We Praise God

We praise God the Father, the Son, and the Holy Spirit.

On most Sundays and special days, we pray:
Glory to God in the highest and peace to his people on earth.

God is good to his people. We want to praise God in words and by what we do.

Draw something you wish to praise God for.

We Ask and God Hears

The priest prays and
asks God to help us.

_____

– – – – – – – – – – –

We say _____ .

Amen

God hears our prayer.
God gives us many blessings.

The Mass

✜ Entrance
  Procession
  and Song
✜ Sign of the Cross
✜ Greeting
✜ Penitential Rite
✜ Glory to God
✜ Opening Prayer

We Remember

What do we celebrate at Mass?
At Mass, we celebrate Jesus'
victory over sin and death.

We Respond

We worship you.
We give you thanks.
We praise you for your glory.

FAMILY CORNER

The Introductory Rites of the Mass give us time
to put aside our daily cares and focus our
attention on God's loving action in our lives.
The entrance procession and song set the spirit
of the celebration. Gathered in Jesus' name, we
ask God and our brothers and sisters to forgive
our sins. We acclaim that Jesus, with the Holy
Spirit, in the glory of God the Father, is Lord of
all creation, and we offer our Opening Prayer.

 Read
Mass Booklet, pages 1–4

Discuss
• how God wants all people to live in peace
  and joy, sharing love and being kind
• how we prepare to celebrate Mass by asking
  forgiveness of God and of one another for
  our failures to show love

 Pray
Glory to God in the highest!

Do
• Talk about how we come to love God and
  others more when we praise what they do
  for us. As a family, discuss how you can
  praise one another.
• Pray the I Confess or the Glory to God with
  your child in the evening until he or she can
  join the people at Mass.
• Help your child to see that actions carry a
  message about what is in our hearts.
  Mention how dressing appropriately for
  Mass, being prompt, and looking at the
  priest and reader when they speak show our
  love for Jesus.

_____

❏ Signature

We Listen to the Word of the Lord

We listen to show respect for those speaking to us. Listening shows that we love and care. We listen carefully when we want to hear.

God speaks to us in the **readings** at Mass.

We listen to God's Word and say:

_____

– – – – – – – – – – – – – – – – – – – –

_____

Thanks be to God.

Copy the missing words on the line.

We pray a **psalm.** We get ready to hear the Gospel. We sing to show our joy:

Color the **alleluia.**

The priest or deacon says: A reading from the holy Gospel according

_____

\- \- \- \- \- \- \- \- \- \- \-

to _____ .
(name of a Gospel)

Copy the words on the lines.

We say:

_____

\- \- \- \- \- \- \- \- \- \- \- \- \- \- \- \- \-

_____

Glory to you, Lord.

The priest or deacon reads the **Gospel.** We listen to the Good News. Then we say:

_____

\- \- \- \- \- \- \- \- \- \- \- \- \- \- \- \- \-

_____

Praise to you, Lord Jesus Christ.

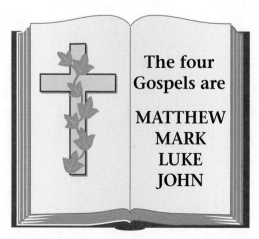

The four Gospels are

MATTHEW
MARK
LUKE
JOHN

The priest or deacon gives a **homily.** He speaks to us about the readings. He helps us to love God and others more.

We Live God's Word

When we hear God's Word at Mass, we find out how we can live as his children.

Here are words from the Bible.

"I was hungry and you gave me food."

Matthew 25:35

Children, obey your parents.

Ephesians 6:1

God loves a cheerful giver.

2 Corinthians 9:7

Draw a line from each sentence to the picture it matches best.

We Tell God
We Believe

**We Believe in
God the Father.**
✠ He is almighty.
✠ He created heaven
and earth.

**We Believe in
Jesus Christ.**
✠ He is God's only Son.
✠ He was born of the
Virgin Mary.
✠ For us he died and
was buried.
✠ On the third day he
rose again.
✠ He will come again.

**We Believe in the
Holy Spirit.**

**We Believe in the
Holy Catholic Church.**

We Believe
that God forgives sins
and that we will rise
from the dead and
live forever.

As Catholic Christians, we believe in Jesus and in what he taught.

When we gather together at Sunday Mass, we pray the **Creed.**

Color the stained-glass window.

We Ask God for Help

These pictures show people with needs. Everyone has needs. What are they?

Jesus cared about people. He helped people who were in need. Jesus' friends helped people in need.

When we love people, we show we care.

At Mass we show we care. We pray for the Church and our country. We pray for the needs of people everywhere and for ourselves.

Write your name and the name of someone you would like to pray for, in the empty spaces.

LORD, HEAR OUR PRAYER

Color the words.

Find the names of the four Gospels. Circle them. (Hint: One is on a slant.)

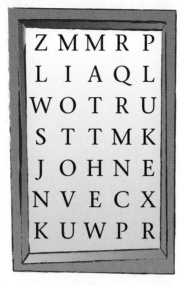

Z M M R P
L I A Q L
W O T R U
S T T M K
J O H N E
N V E C X
K U W P R

Number these parts of the Mass in order.

God Speaks

_____ Psalm

_____ Reading

_____ Gospel

_____ Alleluia

We Speak

_____ Prayer of the Faithful

_____ Creed

The Mass

✛ Reading
✛ Psalm
✛ Alleluia
✛ Gospel
✛ Homily
✛ Creed
✛ Prayer of the Faithful

We Remember

How does God speak to us at Mass?

God speaks to us at Mass through readings from the Bible.

We Respond

Lord, be in my mind, †
on my lips, †
and in my heart. †

FAMILY CORNER

After the Introductory Rites draw us together and prepare us to listen, we hear readings from Scripture. We respond with silent reflection and acclamations. We listen to the homily, relating God's Word to our daily lives. Then we profess our faith. The Creed, a summary of our beliefs, moves us finally to pray for the needs of all.

 Read
Mass Booklet, pages 5–8

Discuss

• the importance of listening with the heart during the readings from the Bible
• the message of Sunday's readings and the homily that explained them
• what you believe about God and the Church
• needs you want to include in the Prayer of the Faithful or your grace before meals

 Pray
Your word, O Lord, is the joy of my heart!

Do

• Make a banner to express your love for God's Word. Display it near your Bible.
• Share favorite Bible stories. Dramatize or illustrate some.
• Prepare a homily on next Sunday's Gospel. Then compare its ideas with those chosen by the priest.
• Invite your child to read a short selection from the Gospels each evening.
• Visit a church with stained-glass windows. Tell the story of each one.

❏ Signature

We Bring Our Gifts

We bring gifts of bread and wine to the altar. We can bring other gifts, like money, too. They are signs of God's goodness to us. They are signs of ourselves. We bring these gifts to show God our love and thanks. We pray that God accepts our sacrifice.

We Give Thanks and Praise

The priest invites us to thank God for his love. God has been very good to us. He made us. He gives us many gifts, but Jesus is the best gift. It is right to give God thanks and praise. The word Eucharist means "giving thanks."

Draw a picture of a gift for which you thank God.

Copy the words on the line with pretty colors.

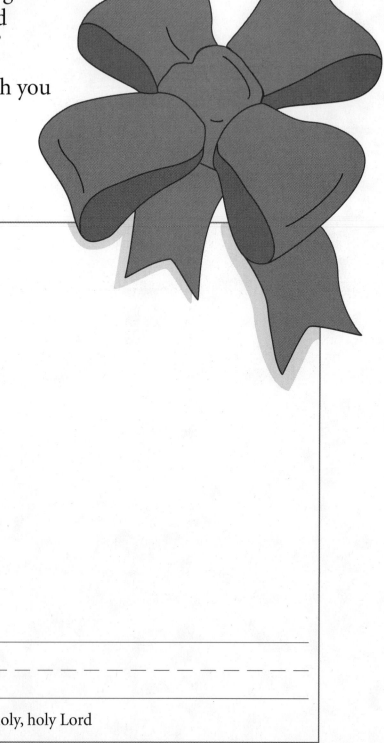

Holy, holy, holy Lord

Draw blue arrows to show what wheat becomes. Draw red arrows to show what grapes become.

 • •

 • •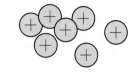

The Body of Jesus • • The Blood of Jesus

Write the missing word:

Blessed be God

_____

— — — — — — — — — —

_____ .

The Mass

✠ Preparation of the Altar and the Gifts
✠ Prayer over the Gifts
✠ Preface
✠ Holy, Holy, Holy

We Remember

What are the bread and wine a sign of?
The bread and wine are a sign of God's goodness and a sign of ourselves.

We Respond

It is right to give him thanks and praise.

FAMILY CORNER

The gifts of bread and wine we bring to the altar at Mass are signs that we want to return to God the gifts of life and love he showers on us.

 Read
Mass Booklet, pages 9–10

Discuss
• how gifts make you feel and how you feel when people show they appreciate your gift
• how you contribute to the collection at Mass to show you are giving yourself to God

 Pray
Blessed be God forever!

Do
• Make a family banner for your child's First Communion.
• Visit a bakery with your child to see how bread is made.
• Volunteer to carry the gifts at Sunday Mass.
• Review your family practice of praying at meals.
• Read *A Birthday Party for Frances* by Russell Hoban or *Mr. Rabbit and the Lovely Present* by Charlotte Zolotow to lead into a discussion of gift giving.

❑ Signature

Jesus Gives Himself as a Sacrifice at Mass

The priest does what Jesus did at the Last Supper. He says:

> This is my Body, which will be given up for you. This is the cup of my Blood. It will be shed for you.

Eucharistic Prayer

Our gift of bread and wine becomes Jesus. Jesus is with us.

Jesus is the perfect sacrifice.

He offers himself to his Father with love. He offers himself for us.

Jesus told us to remember him.

We remember:
   Christ has died,
   Christ is risen,
   Christ will come again.

We say:

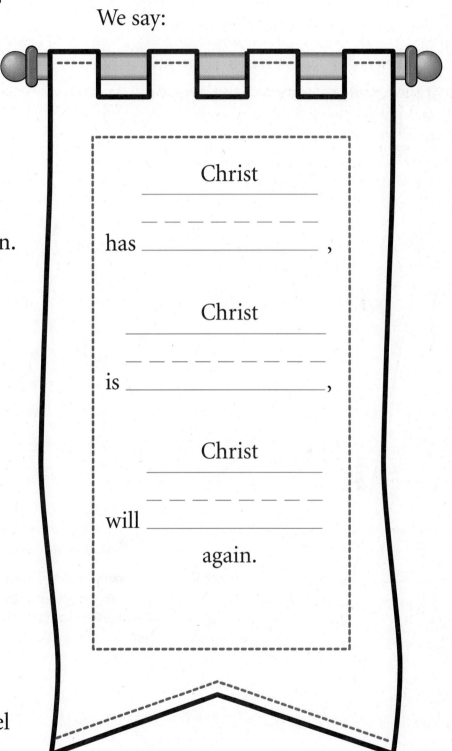

Christ
_____
_ _ _ _ _ _ _ _ _ _

has _____ ,

Christ
_____
_ _ _ _ _ _ _ _ _ _

is _____ ,

Christ
_____
_ _ _ _ _ _ _ _ _ _

will _____

again.

Fill in the blanks. Decorate the banner. Make fringe and a tassel for it.

We Offer Ourselves with Jesus

The priest offers Jesus to God our Father. We offer Jesus with the priest. We offer ourselves with Jesus.

We listen as the priest offers our gifts. Then he lifts up the host and the chalice. He praises the Father. We sing or say **yes** to everything he said:

Color the Great Amen. Decorate it.

Jesus Gives Himself to the Father

Number the pictures in order.

◯ on the cross   ◯ at the Last Supper

◯ at the Eucharist today

We Remember

What is the perfect sacrifice?

Jesus is the perfect sacrifice who offers himself at Mass.

We Respond

My Lord and my God!

FAMILY CORNER

In the Eucharistic Prayer of the Mass, we join Christ in praising and thanking the Father for all he has done for us. We unite our sacrifice with Christ's and stand with him before the Father, open to his transforming love.

 Read
Mass Booklet, pages 11–16

Discuss
• how the greatest gift of love is the gift of self
• what Jesus has done to show he loves us

 Pray
Father, I adore you!

Do
• Remind your child when it is time for the Great Amen at Mass so that he or she can respond.
• Help your child learn the Memorial Acclamations found on page 13 of the Mass Booklet.
• Encourage your child's efforts to love others as Jesus loves them. Praise acts of sharing, kindness, and patience. Let your child know that these are ways of letting Jesus live in him or her.

_____

❏ Signature

We Prepare to Receive Jesus

We pray the **Our Father** to ask forgiveness and to show we are all brothers and sisters in God's family.

We give one another a **sign of peace** and say:
  Peace be with you.

We ask Jesus to forgive us for the times we have upset the peace of God's family. We say:
   Lamb of God, you take
      away the sins of the world: have
      mercy on us.
The priest breaks the bread.

We think of the great love of Jesus and of our weak love. We look at the host and say:
      Lord, I am not worthy to
      receive you.

Jesus Helps a Roman Soldier

Reader: The servant of a Roman soldier was sick in bed. The soldier loved his servant and took good care of him. The soldier went to Jesus to ask for help.

Soldier: Sir, my servant is very sick. He needs your help.

Jesus: I am very sorry to hear that. I will come and heal him.

Soldier *(kneeling)*: Lord, I am not worthy to have you enter under my roof. Only say the word and my servant will be healed.

Jesus *(lifting the soldier to his feet)*: You have great faith. As you have believed, let it be done for you.

Soldier: Thank you. I know that it will be done.

Reader: At that moment the servant was healed. The soldier's family was happy and rejoiced with him.

adapted from Matthew 8:5–13

Fill in the missing words. Use the Word Bank.

This story shows us how to prepare for

_____

_ _

_____ .

When Jesus comes to us, he

_____

_ _ _ _ _ _ _ _ _ _ _ _

will _____ us.

We will say, "Lord, I am

_____

_ _ _ _ _ _ _ _ _ _ _ _

not _____ to

receive you, but only say

_____   _____

_ _ _ _ _ _ _ _ _ _ _ _   _ _ _ _ _ _ _ _ _ _ _ _

the _____ and I shall be _____ ."

Word Bank

worthy

healed

help

word

Holy Communion

Jesus Comes to Us in Holy Communion

We have tried to love as Jesus does. We have fasted for an hour from everything except water and medicine. Now we are ready to receive him.

We pray and sing while we wait. When it is our turn, the priest or another person shows us the host and says, "The Body of Christ." We answer, "Amen."

If we receive from the cup, "The Blood of Christ" is said. We answer, "Amen."

We Thank Jesus for the Gift of Himself

The time after Communion is holy. We
are united with Jesus and his family. Jesus
is within us. Jesus, who loves us and who
is so good, has given us himself. We speak
to Jesus in our hearts. We can tell him
anything we wish.

We can say:
Jesus,
      I adore you.
      I love you.
      I thank you.
      I ask you . . .
      I resolve to . . .

What do the blue letters spell?

_____

– – – – – – – – – – – – – – – – – –

_____

This word will help you know what to say
after Communion.

Sometimes we pray and sing our thanks to
God together.

The Mass

- Our Father
- Sign of Peace
- Lamb of God
- Lord, I Am Not Worthy
- Communion
- Thanksgiving after Communion

Write what you say on the lines.

The Body of Christ.

_____

– – – – – – – – – –

Amen.

The Blood of Christ.

_____

– – – – – – – – – –

Amen.

Use your bottom hand to pick up the host and put it into your mouth. (Your hands should be clean.) Or put your tongue out far enough to receive the host.

We Remember

Who comes to us in Holy Communion?
Jesus comes to us in Holy Communion.

What do we do after receiving Holy Communion?
We speak to Jesus in our hearts. We thank him in prayer and song.

We Respond

Lord, I am not worthy to receive you, but only say the word and I shall be healed.

FAMILY CORNER

Those parts of the Mass that lead directly to Communion prepare us to receive the Body and Blood of the Lord as our spiritual food and drink. The celebrant breaks the bread as Jesus did at the Last Supper, so that we may receive him, who gives himself and his life for us.

Read
Mass Booklet, pages 17–22

Discuss
- what Holy Communion means to you
- how to use the moments before and after receiving Communion to sing or to pray short prayers such as, "Come, Lord Jesus!"
- how your child can begin using the time after Communion for personal prayer. See pages 21–22 of the Mass Booklet.
- how we prepare for Holy Communion by fasting (Tell your child never to chew gum during Mass.)

Pray
Come, Lord Jesus, come.

Do
- At bedtime, pray with your child prayers he or she composes to express the desire to receive Jesus in Holy Communion.
- Help your child learn the Lamb of God and the Lord, I Am Not Worthy on pages 18–19 of the Mass Booklet.
- Practice with your child how to receive Communion. Tell your child that, to receive Communion in the hand, he or she should reach up and out toward the minister to show a desire for Jesus.

_____

❏ Signature

We Love and Serve the Lord

Jesus loved and served God our Father. He sent his apostles out to do this too. He sent them to share God's love.

The apostles went out and helped people. They taught the people about God. They taught the people how to love God and one another.

The priest takes the place of Jesus at Mass. He blesses us and sends us out to do what Jesus and the apostles did:

Go in peace to love and serve the Lord.

We answer:

Thanks be to God.

We Love and Serve the Lord in Many Places

We love and serve God's people everywhere.

Match the pictures and the words.
Put the correct letter in each box.

A. at home **D.** on the street
B. at school **E.** in the world
C. on the
playground

Draw yourself bringing Jesus' love to others.

Some hosts from Mass are kept in the **tabernacle.** In this **Blessed Sacrament** Jesus is always with us in our churches. He can be brought to sick people at any time, and we can visit him. We can thank Jesus for the gift of himself. We can tell him that we love him too.

We Celebrate the Eucharist

Put the letter of the sentence that tells about the picture on each line.

A. We receive Jesus in Holy Communion and become one with God's family.

B. We listen to God speak to us.

C. The bread and wine become Jesus.

D. We bring gifts as signs of ourselves.

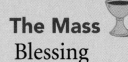
Draw a smile 🙂 if the answer is yes.

Draw a frown 🙁 if the answer is no.

○ **1.** Did Jesus give us the Mass at the Last Supper?

○ **2.** Do we pretend that bread and wine are Jesus at Mass?

○ **3.** Do Jewish people celebrate God's love at Passover?

○ **4.** Does the Bible say that Jesus fed a crowd with a few loaves and fish?

○ **5.** Did Jesus wash the apostles' feet to teach us how to love?

○ **6.** Did Jesus offer himself to make up for his sins?

○ **7.** Are we worthy to receive Holy Communion?

○ **8.** Can we offer Jesus and ourselves to the Father at Mass?

○ **9.** Does God speak to us through the readings at Mass?

○ **10.** Is a sacrifice a gift given to God?

We Remember

What may the priest say at the end of Mass?

The priest may say, "Go in peace to love and serve the Lord."

We Respond

Thanks be to God.

FAMILY CORNER

After time for thanksgiving, the celebrant concludes our communion moment with a prayer. Then, in the dismissal rite of the Mass, he invokes God's blessing and sends us out to do what we have promised: to love and serve God and to enrich the lives of others.

 Read
Mass Booklet, page 23

Discuss
- practical ways your child can bring more joy, friendship, and beauty to the world
- what you are trying to do to bring Jesus' Spirit to your world at home and work
- how kind deeds are a fitting thanksgiving for Holy Communion

 Pray
Help me love and serve you, Lord!

Do
- Continue to use the Mass Booklet to review the parts of the Mass.
- Each week after Mass, decide on a way you as a family can help someone in need.
- Name a part of the Mass. Take turns telling something about it.
- Hold the family celebration (see the next page) before your child's First Holy Communion.

❑ Signature

115

A Family Celebration of Bread

Parent: *(When the family is gathered around a bare table, unfold a tablecloth and place it on the table along with a loaf of bread, butter, and jelly.)*

We are together at the same table, all children of God our Father. As a sign of the love that unites us, we shall share this bread. *(Break bread into pieces, which all eat together.)*

How good it is to share the same bread! It would not be the same if we each ate our pieces of bread alone. This bread that we have eaten together is ordinary bread. Let us think of the Mass, where those who believe in Jesus share the Bread of Life. Soon we will have the privilege of sharing it with *[name of child]*.

Let us listen to the Word of God.

Reading

I am the living bread that came down from heaven;
whoever eats this bread will live forever; and the
bread that I will give is my flesh for the life of the world.
John 6:51

I give you a new commandment: love one another.
As I have loved you, so you also should love one another.
John 13:34

Older Child or Parent: Jesus becomes Living Bread to help us love God our Father and each other as he loves us.

First Communicant: Jesus, I want to love others as you love them. Come and help me to love and obey my parents. Help me to love my brothers and sisters. Help me to be kind to all people. Help me to show that I love you and your heavenly Father.

Activity

Discuss different ways to please God at home: during meals, in the morning before school, after school, and in the evening.

Song

Sing together some of the First Communion songs.

Honoring the Eucharist

Long ago the Blessed Sacrament was sometimes carried in procession through the town to bless the people, into the fields to bless the land and the crops, and even into battles and disasters. Today the Ortiz family in Mexico looks forward each year to the feast of the Body and Blood of Christ, formerly called Corpus Christi. For this feast the family members join their neighborhood priests and friends in a grand outdoor procession. Maria Ortiz helps her mother set up an altar near their house. They cover it with fine linen. Her father practices the trumpet because he will be playing in the band that day.

On the feast day, priests in their finest vestments and people in their finest clothes walk behind the Eucharist contained in a gold and jeweled monstrance. The priest stops at the small altars along the way and blesses the people with the monstrance. Little Roberto Ortiz claps and squeals with joy at the fireworks that add to the celebration.

In Spain, France, Italy, and Portugal on Corpus Christi, people use flower petals to make elaborate designs on the streets for the procession to walk over. In Austria decorated boats carry the Eucharist across lakes, while worshipers follow in small boats.

In the United States this feast is on the Sunday after Trinity Sunday, usually in June. Now that your child has received First Communion, you may wish to celebrate this day at home in one of these ways:

✣ Bake bread together and recall each family member's First Communion, bringing out pictures, prayerbooks, and any other mementos of the day.
✣ Participate in Mass as a family and afterwards have a festive breakfast.
✣ Make a family visit to the Blessed Sacrament.

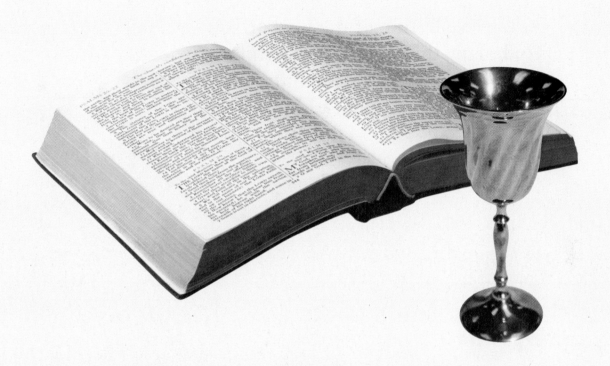

You might also begin the tradition of having a family blessing cup. Purchase or make a cup to be used only on special occasions. At the beginning of the meal, fill the cup with a beverage. Read a Scripture passage suited to the occasion and then pray petitions asking for certain blessings. Pass the cup around the table for all to share. Close the ritual with a prayer said in common, such as the Our Father.

Sacrifices

At the celebration of the Eucharist we offer
God many things. Help your child draw or
paste pictures of what we offer. Include Jesus,
ourselves, bread, wine, and our work.

The Church Celebrates God's Care

This unit introduces the children to ways in which the Church celebrates God's care and Christ's presence in the world today. The children learn how each Church member helps carry out God's plan and how Church leaders guide us to follow Jesus more closely.

The Church Is the Body of Christ

The Church is like a human body. It has a head and many parts, but it is one body. It is the Body of Christ. Jesus is the head.

Each Christian is a part of the Body of Christ. Each one helps the Church in a special way. In the Eucharist, Jesus helps us to be one.

The Church Brings People to Jesus

Jesus said, "I am the good shepherd.
I have other sheep that do not belong
to this fold. These also I must lead. There
will be one flock, one shepherd."

John 10:14, 16

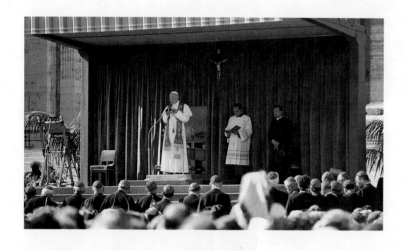

Jesus has chosen good
shepherds for his Church.

✤ The **Holy Father** is the chief shepherd.
He teaches all people about God's love.

Our pope is named _____.

✤ **Bishops** around the world help the Holy Father.

Our bishop is named _____.

✤ **Priests** help bishops.

Our pastor is named _____.

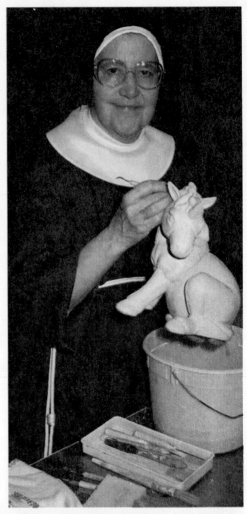

Deacons, brothers, sisters, and priests who are religious follow Jesus in a special way. Some religious serve in parishes. Some spend their days praying for the Church. Some work as **missionaries** and spread the Good News near and far. All of them bring Jesus' love to many people.

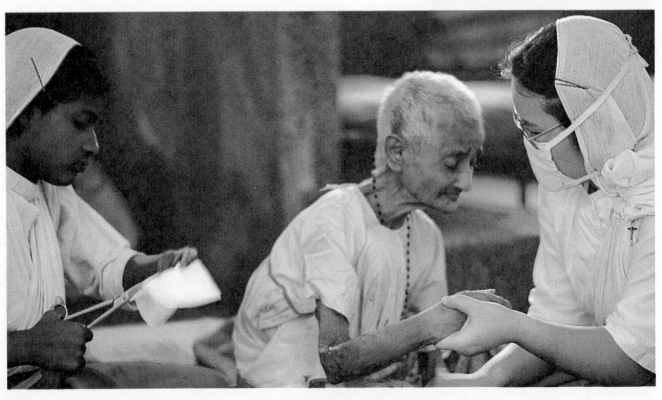

All members of the Church help others know Jesus' love. Boys and girls can help too.

Read the sentences. Find the missing words in the flowers and print them on the lines.

This girl is making a

_____

- - - - - - - - -

_____

person happy.

This boy is showing God's loving care to a

_____

- - - - - - -

_____ child.

This boy may be praying

_____

- - - - -

for _____ people.

These children are bringing Jesus' joy to a

_____

- - - - - - -

_____ person.

sick

little

lonely

all

We Become like Jesus

Since we are one with Jesus, we must become like him. John Bosco helped others to be one with Jesus. He started the **Happy Company Club.**

It has two rules:

1. Never do anything that a child of God should not do.
2. Be cheerful about whatever you do.

Print H.C.C. under the picture if you think the child in it belongs to the **Happy Company Club.**

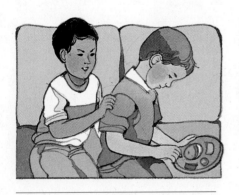

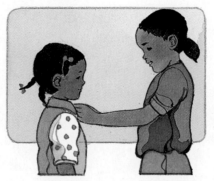

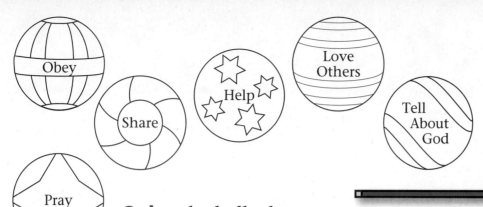

Color the balls that tell what members of the Body of Christ do.

The Eucharist gives us power to live like Christ.

We Remember

What is the Body of Christ?
The Church is the Body of Christ. Jesus is the head and we are the members.

We Respond

Jesus, make me more like you.

FAMILY CORNER

The Church is one body in Christ. Christ is the head, and Christians are the members. The Eucharist unites all the members and enables us to make our lives an expression of Christ's love. The Church is missionary by nature. Through prayer and service, each member can share Christ's message with others.

Read
Corinthians 12:20–27

Discuss
- how a body suffers when even one part is hurt
- how the Church is healthy and able to show Christ's love to the world only when the members are one in love
- how Jesus showed love for others
- ways your family can share God's love with people near and far

 Pray
Thy kingdom come!

Do
- Ask your child to share the story of John Bosco and the Happy Company Club. Then tell something each person in the family does that would make her or him qualify as a member of the club.
- Talk about the difficulties you face as Catholics and ask Jesus for strength to meet them.
- Decide on a sacrifice your family will make to help feed starving children.
- Pray that priests, deacons, and brother and sister religious may be good leaders.
- Share something a person said or did that brought you closer to God.

❏ Signature

123

Mary Asks Jesus to Help

Reader: Jesus and his apostles went to a wedding. Mary, the mother of Jesus, was there.

Everyone had a good time, but soon there was no more wine. Mary saw this and went to Jesus.

Mary: Son, they have no more wine.

Reader: Then she called the waiters.

Mary: Do whatever Jesus tells you.

Jesus: Fill the jars with water. Then give some to the chief waiter.

Reader: The waiter tasted it. It wasn't water anymore but wine.

Waiter: You have saved the best wine until last!

adapted from John 2:1–10

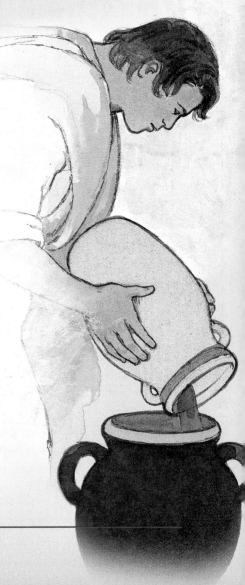

Color the picture of Mary, Mother of God. Think about her love for you.

Who is the Mother of the Church?
Mary is the Mother of the Church.

We Respond

Mary, help of Christians, pray for us.

FAMILY CORNER

History abounds with stories of people who have experienced Mary's help. Mary, Mother of the Church, intercedes for her children and leads them to Jesus. Devotion to her brings us ever closer to her Son.

 Read
John 2:1–11

Discuss
- how you feel when someone helps you without waiting to be asked
- ways people show they care about others
- some needs for which you want to invoke Mary's help

 Pray
Mary, help of Christians, pray for us!

Do
- Prepare a shrine for Mary and decorate it with flowers and candles.
- Pray together each day the Consecration to Mary that is inside the back cover of this book.
- Plan a celebration to honor Mary, Help of Christians.
- Share stories of how you experienced Mary's intercessory power.

❏ Signature

126

We Love God and Others

Find the Way to Heaven

Follow the path. The letters tell how to get to heaven. Print them.

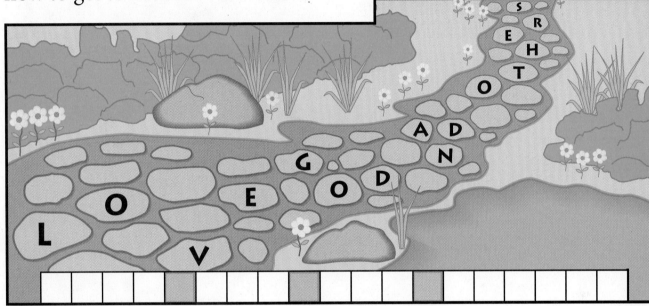

Print the missing words in these sentences. They tell us things we can do to show our love for God. (Use the code to find the letters that belong in each box.) Then read the sentences.

C	E	H	I	K	N	O	S	T
1	2	3	4	5	6	7	8	9

9	3	4	6	5

often about God.

1	3	7	7	8	2

to do what is right.

We Can Meet Jesus Today

Jesus loves us. He is always with us. He is most with us in the Church. He is in his Word. He is with us in a special way when we pray and during Mass.

Pick a Word

The sentences here tell us things we can do to be with Jesus.

Print the words that are missing. You can find them in the tree.

Listen

Love

Pray

Bible

Holy

Mary

Obey

Sorry

1. P __ __ __ each day.

2. Read the B __ __ __ __.

3. Ask M __ __ __ to pray for us.

4. Be s __ __ __ __ for sins.

5. L __ __ __ __ __ when the Bible is read at Mass.

6. Receive Jesus in H __ __ __ Communion.

7. O __ __ __ our parents.

8. Ask the Holy Spirit to fill our hearts with l __ __ __ .

Use the words in the Word Bank to complete Jesus' promise.

"I am the _____ bread that

came down from _____.

Whoever _____ this bread

will live _____ . The bread

that I will give is my _____

for the _____ of the world."

adapted from John 6:51

Word Bank

life   flesh   heaven   eats

living   food   forever

We Remember

What do Christians do?
Christians try to love God and others as Jesus did.
How do we know Jesus is with us?
Jesus said, "I am with you always."

We Respond

Glory to the Father, and to the Son, and to the Holy Spirit: as it was in the beginning, is now, and will be forever. Amen.

FAMILY CORNER

God cares for us through his Church and calls each member of the Church to glorify him. Our prayers and good deeds show our love.

Read
Ephesians 4:11–16

Discuss
• times when you realized that Jesus shared your sorrow
• ways your family shows God's loving care to your relatives and neighbors
• how God has cared for us through priests and other members of the Church.

Pray
Glory to the Father, and to the Son, and to the Holy Spirit!

Do
• Take turns saying words of Jesus.
• Help your child keep a diary with a sentence or picture showing a sign of God's care each day or week.
• Use Family Corner suggestions during vacation.
• Discuss the "I Love God and Others" section in the Notes to Parents at the beginning of this book.

❏ Signature

We Celebrate God's Loving Care

Song

Leader: When we were baptized, we became members of the Body of Christ, the Church. Because we belong to the Church, we met Jesus in the Sacrament of Reconciliation. We became one with him and others in Holy Communion. Today we thank Jesus for the signs of his love. We pray that all people will know and love Jesus.

Priest: God our Father, look with love on your people. Pour out upon us your gifts so that we may lead others to you. We ask this through Christ our Lord.

All: Amen.

Readings

There is one Lord, one faith, one Baptism, and one God who is Father of all. Each of us has been given gifts to serve the Body of Christ. Jesus wants us to be one in what we believe about him. When each person does what God wants, the whole body grows. It becomes filled with love.

adapted from Ephesians 4:5, 11–16

The Word of the Lord.

All: Thanks be to God.

Song

Priest: A reading from the holy Gospel according to John.

All: Glory to you, Lord.

Priest: Jesus looked up into heaven and prayed: "Father, make those you have given me true believers in you. As you sent me into the world, I have sent them to the whole world.

I pray not only for these apostles, but for all those who listen to their words and believe in me. May my followers be so completely one that the world will realize it was you who sent me and that you have loved them as much as you love me."

adapted from John 17:18–23

The Gospel of the Lord.

All: Praise to you, Lord Jesus Christ!

Profession of Faith

Sing "We Believe" or recite the Creed on page 91.

Priest: Lord, we pray for these children who believe in you. May they enjoy the gift of your love, share it with others, and spread it everywhere. We ask this in the name of Jesus the Lord.

Intercessions

Leaders: Now that we have been blessed, let us turn to our Father in heaven, ask him to listen to our prayers, and say, "Father, hear our prayer."

For the Holy Father, bishops, priests, deacons, and all who belong to the Church, that we may live joyfully as Christians. *[Response]*

For all the people of the world, that we may live as brothers and sisters who care about one another . . .

For our brothers and sisters who are hungry, sick, or in need, that our prayers and sacrifices may help them . . .

For those who do not yet believe in Jesus, that we may show them his love . . .

For those who have sinned, that they may turn to God for forgiveness . . .

For all of us, that we may share God's love with one another . . .

Priest: Father, we have come before you with faith and love. Hear our prayers and let your Church serve you in peace and joy. We ask this through Christ our Lord.

Song

Do You Know the Answers?

Here are some questions and answers that you should know from your study of **God Cares for Us.** When you can answer each question for your parents without help, color in the space under the number.

(1) Why does God make every person in his image and likeness?

God makes every person in his image and likeness because he loves each one.

Chapter 1

(2) How do we know God loves us very much?

We know God loves us because he sent his Son, Jesus, to save us from sin.

Chapter 2

(3) When did we receive a share in God's life?

We received a share in God's life when we were baptized.

Chapter 3

(4) Why did Jesus give us his Church?

Jesus gave us his Church so that we could share his life now and forever in heaven.

Chapter 3

(5) Who belongs to the Church?

Everyone who believes in Jesus and is baptized belongs to the Church.

Chapter 3

(6) What are the two great commandments?

The two great commandments are
"Love God with all your heart" and
"Love your neighbor as you love yourself."

Chapter 5

7 **How do we show our love for God?**
We show we love God when we pray, say his name with love, and celebrate his day. *Chapter 5*

8 **How do we show our love for others?**
We show our love for others when we are obedient, kind, pure, honest, and truthful. *Chapter 7*

9 **Does God forgive us when we are sorry for our sins?**
God always forgives us when we are sorry for our sins. *Chapter 9*

10 **What is sin?**
Sin is failing to love God by choosing to say no to what we know God wants us to do. *Chapter 10*

11 **How can we show our love for God after we sin?**
We can show our love for God after we sin by saying that we are sorry and making up our minds not to sin again. *Chapter 11*

12 **How does the Holy Spirit help us?**
The Holy Spirit helps us to love God and others as Jesus does. The Spirit calls us to forgiveness when we have sinned. *Chapter 11*

13 **Why does Jesus invite us to celebrate the Sacrament of Reconciliation?**
Jesus invites us to celebrate the Sacrament of Reconciliation so that he can forgive us through the priest and give us peace. *Chapter 12*

14 **What is the most important thing we do in the Sacrament of Reconciliation?**

Being sorry for having offended God is the most important thing we do in the Sacrament of Reconciliation. *Chapter 13*

15 **How does Jesus give us himself as food and drink?**

Jesus gives us himself as food and drink when we receive him in Holy Communion. *Chapter 15*

16 **When did Jesus offer himself for us in the Eucharist?**

Jesus first offered himself in the Eucharist at the Last Supper. He gave his life for us on the cross and offers himself to his Father for us at every Mass. *Chapter 16*

17 **Why do we take part in Sunday Mass?**

We take part in Sunday Mass to hear God's Word, to offer Jesus and ourselves to the Father, and to receive Jesus in Holy Communion. *Chapter 16*

18 **How long do we fast from food and drink before Holy Communion?**

We do not eat or drink anything except water or medicine for one hour before Holy Communion. *Chapter 21*

19 **How do we thank Jesus for sharing his life with us?**

We thank Jesus for sharing his life with us by trying to live like him even when this is hard to do. *Chapter 22*

20 **Why is Mary the Mother of the Church?**

Mary is the Mother of the Church because she is the mother of Jesus and he gave her to us. She shows us how to be like him. *Chapter 24*

FAMILY FEATURE

A Remembering Circle

At least once a year the Thomas family members gather for a remembering circle. This is an African-American custom that helps them understand their life history and see that our lives are woven together. We are all interdependent in living the Christian life.

The Thomas children, James and Jason, arrange cushions or chairs in a circle in the family room. Mrs. Thomas makes a beautiful flower arrangement and sets it in the center of the circle along with a candle. Last fall she put branches of colorful leaves in a vase and made a circle of small vigil lights around it.

In the evening everyone in the family sits in the circle in the candlelight and thinks about people in their lives who have given them beautiful memories. These are people who have called forth their giftedness or those who have supported them by giving good advice, a shoulder to cry on, or a helping hand. They can be living or deceased, relatives, friends, or neighbors. Mrs. Thomas usually recalls something about her deceased grandmother, whom she affectionately calls "M'dear." This year Jason thought about Saint Anthony who helped him find his dog Spunky when Spunky had run away.

Mr. Thomas remembered the doctor who set his broken leg and the friends who visited him in the hospital. Anyone who wishes may share a "remembering." After each remembering, the whole group prays, "We remember you in love for these good memories."

You might begin the family tradition of a remembering circle in order to become more aware of what it means to belong to the Communion of Saints, the Church. It would be a good way to begin or end your family celebration of a holiday like Thanksgiving or New Year's Day.

The Church

Write the names or draw or paste pictures of Church members in the stones below. You might include Mary, the pope, your bishop, grandparents, favorite saints, and yourselves.

SUPPLEMENT

John the Baptist Was Chosen by God

Print the baby's name on the line:

_____

- - - - - - - - - -

John

Zechariah's Song

You, child, will be called prophet of the Most High, for you will go before the Lord to prepare his ways.

adapted from Luke 1:76

Sharing Advent as a Family

Advent is a joyful time for preparing our hearts to celebrate Jesus' birth. The same Jesus who was born in Bethlehem many years ago desires to live in the world today through us.

Our Advent prayers and practices can make us more aware of his presence in ourselves and others. Set aside time each evening to build a spirit of joyful longing for Jesus to be born anew in your hearts. Decide how you as a family can make each day of Advent a time of special preparation for the celebration of Christmas. One activity you can work on together as a family is building a manger scene.

1. Cut out the figures from the tear-out sheet near the back of this book.

2. Form a base for each figure by gluing together the ends of strips of paper 5 inches by 1/2 inch. Then glue the bottom of the figures to the base.

3. Decide whether to build the scene all at once or set one figure in place each day. You may make a stable or other background and add other figures.

4. Read a Scripture passage as each figure is added to the scene. Then discuss its meaning for you as you prepare to welcome Jesus more fully into your family life. Suggested readings follow.

Lamb Bible Reading: John 10:14–15, 27–28
Think of God's love in sending us Jesus, and pray:
The LORD is my shepherd; there is nothing I lack. (Psalm 23:1)

Shepherd Bible Reading: Luke 2:8–10
Think of ways God speaks to you, and pray:
Speak, for your servant is listening. (1 Samuel 3:10)

Mary Bible Reading: Luke 1:26–28
Imagine how Mary felt, and pray:
O Mary, help us prepare our hearts for Jesus.
Hail Mary . . .

Joseph Bible Reading: Luke 2:1–5
Think of how Joseph followed God's plan with trust, and pray:
I . . . trust in God's faithful love forever. (Psalm 52:10)

Jesus Bible Reading: Luke 2:11–14
Thank God for Jesus, and say or sing:
Come, Lord Jesus. Come and be born in our hearts.

Wise Men Bible Reading: Matthew 2:1–11
Thank God for leading you to Jesus, and adore him as you say or sing:
O come, let us adore him.

Reader: After the Last Supper, Jesus went to a garden to pray. Soldiers came and led Jesus away to prison.

The next day Jesus had to carry a big cross up the hill to Calvary. Jesus was nailed to the cross. Some people made fun of him.

People: If you are the King of the Jews, come down from the cross. Save yourself!

Reader: At noon the sun stopped shining. It grew very dark.

Jesus prayed for those who hurt him.

Jesus: Father, forgive them. They do not know what they are doing.

Reader: At about three o'clock, Jesus spoke to his Father.

Jesus: Father, it is finished. I give myself to you.

Reader: Then Jesus bowed his head and died. Jesus offered the sacrifice of his life for us. Jesus showed his great love for his Father and for us.

On the third day, Jesus rose from the dead. He won a victory over sin and death. We can live forever in heaven with him.

We can make little sacrifices during Lent to thank Jesus for his love.

We Remember

What is Lent?
Lent is a special time to show Jesus, our Savior, how much we love him.

We Respond

All for you, O Jesus.

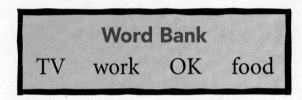

Word Bank

TV   work   OK   food

Fill in the words that are missing in these sentences.

_____

We can eat _____ we don't like.

_____

We can do our best _____ in school.

_____

We can give up a _____ program to help someone.

_____

We can say _____ when we cannot have what we want.

Sharing Lent as a Family

Ash Wednesday. Talk about Lent as a time when Christians change some things in their lives in order to become more Christlike. Give the family members small pieces of paper and let them write one thing they would like to improve in, or eliminate from, their lives. Place the pieces of paper in a foil pan and have an adult burn the papers. Then let each family member use the ashes to make a cross on another's forehead, asking God to bless the efforts to change. Conclude with spontaneous prayer or the Our Father.

The Pretzel. The pretzel—made from only flour, water, and salt—reminds us that long ago during Lent the people fasted from milk, butter, eggs, cheese, cream, and meat. They made the small breads we call pretzels and shaped them into the form of arms crossed in prayer. Serve this Lenten food frequently during this season as a reminder that Lent is a time for special prayer as well as a time for fasting.

Caring for a Seed or Bulb. Planting some seeds or bulbs and taking care of them during the weeks of Lent can help your family understand better the death/new-life theme of Lent. At Easter arrange the plants with other "new life" symbols, such as eggs or butterflies.

Sacrifice. Sacrifice, a word commonly associated with Lent, is derived from two Latin words that mean "to make holy." Prayerful reflection and family discussion of Isaiah 58:1–9 can help your family decide how to respond more fully to the Lord through Lenten sacrifices.

Many families eat a poverty meal once a week during Lent and donate the savings from this meal and their other Lenten sacrifices to groups devoted to the missions or to the liberation of the oppressed and powerless. Many parishes participate in Operation Rice Bowl.

Passion (Palm) Sunday. The palms we receive in church on the last Sunday of Lent remind us that when Christ our King entered Jerusalem the people acclaimed him and waved palms in welcome. Have a procession during which you place blessed palms in each room of your home, saying, "Praise and honor to you, Lord Jesus Christ, King of endless glory." Have your family repeat the acclamation. End your procession with a discussion of what your family will do to celebrate Holy Week.

Easter Vigil. Easter is not simply one feast among many. It is the feast of the year and can be truly celebrated as such by those who have prepared their hearts during Lent. Decorate your table with a baptismal robe and candle. Renew your baptismal promises as a family and talk about the paschal candle that will be seen in church at Mass on Easter and during the Easter season.

Missionaries Spread God's Word of Love

St. Thérèse was a missionary in the Church, although she never left her convent.

She prayed and made sacrifices for people all over the world.

We too can be missionaries and spread God's love by our prayers and sacrifices.

We can ask St. Thérèse to help us.

Ask God to bless all people.

We Remember

Whom does Jesus love?
Jesus loves everyone in the world.

We Respond

Holy Mary, pray for us and for all the children of the world.

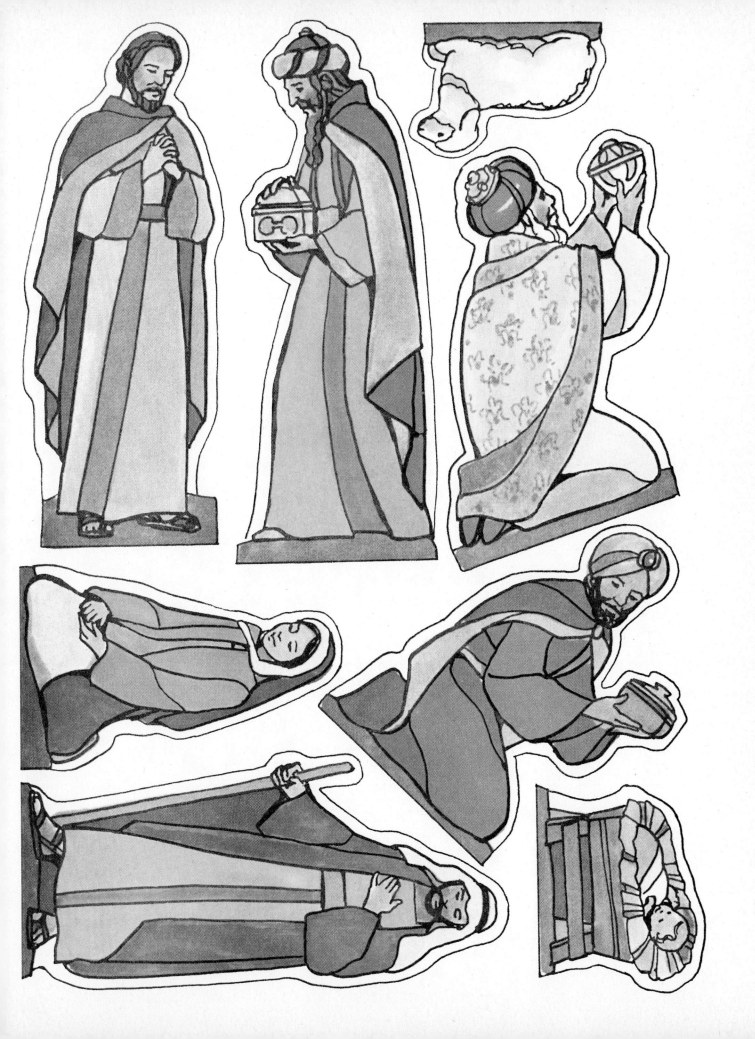

O Come, O Come, Emmanuel

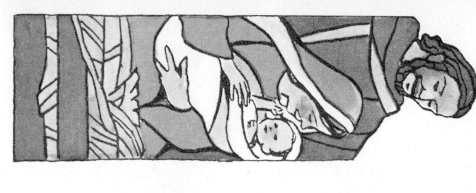

O come, O come, Emmanuel,
And ransom captive Israel
That mourns in lonely exile here
Until the Son of God appear.

Rejoice! Rejoice! O Israel,
To you shall come Emmanuel.

Hail Mary

Hail Mary, full of grace!
The Lord is with you;
Blessed are you among women,
And blessed is the fruit
of your womb, Jesus.

Holy Mary, Mother of God,
Pray for us sinners, now
and at the hour of our death.

Amen.

Fold here

O Little Town of Bethlehem

by Phillips Brooks

O little town of Bethlehem,
How still we see thee lie!
Above thy deep and dreamless sleep
The silent stars go by.

Yet in thy dark streets shineth
The everlasting Light;
The hopes and fears of all the years
Are met in thee tonight.

O holy Child of Bethlehem,
Descend to us we pray.

Cast out our sin and enter in;
Be born in us today.

We hear the Christmas angels
The great glad tidings tell;
O, come to us, abide with us,
Our Lord Emmanuel!

Hark, the Herald Angels Sing

Hark, the herald angels sing,
"Glory to the newborn King;

Peace on earth, and mercy mild,
God and sinners reconciled."

Joyful all ye nations rise,
Join the triumph of the skies.

With angelic hosts proclaim,
"Christ is born in Bethlehem."

Hark, the herald angels sing,
"Glory to the newborn King."

Silent Night!

Franz Grüber, Joseph Mohr

Silent night, holy night.
All is calm, all is bright.

'Round yon Virgin Mother and Child.
Holy infant, so tender and mild.

Sleep in heavenly peace,
Sleep in heavenly peace.

Silent night, holy night.
Shepherds quake at the sight.

Glories stream from heaven afar.
Heavenly hosts sing Alleluia.

Christ, the Savior, is born!
Christ, the Savior, is born!

You are
invited.

Fold

Cut on this line

Dear _____ ,

You are invited to prepare to receive Jesus in Holy Communion.

God's people would like you to join them at the table of the Lord.

You will be enrolled at a special celebration to be held at _____ at _____ o'clock.

on _____

Please come.

Please sign the form and return it to your teacher to let me know if you will be here.

In Christ,

_____

Dear Father _____ ,

I am happy to be a Catholic Christian.

I would like to prepare to receive Jesus in Holy Communion.

I will try to prepare well.

I will be at the celebration.

_____

_ _

_____

Make an Easter Basket of Love for Jesus

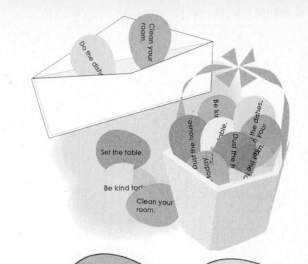

- ✠ Use an egg cup from an egg carton.
- ✠ Glue on a piece of ribbon for a handle.
- ✠ Cut out or have someone else help you cut out the eggs and place them in an envelope.
- ✠ Put the basket in your room.
- ✠ Each morning after you pray, take an egg from the envelope and read it. Place it in front of your basket.
- ✠ Make the sacrifice during the day to show love for Jesus.
- ✠ After your night prayers, put the egg in the basket. If you forget to make the sacrifice, put the egg back in the envelope.

Thank Jesus for dying on the cross.

Help someone today.

Say something kind to someone.

Say the Our Father for the poor.

Fill an Easter Basket with Love for Jesus

Obey at home.

Do the dishes.

Make someone happy.

Do the dishes.

Eat all your food at mealtime.

Show someone you care about him or her.

Help around the house.

Give in to others.

Tell Jesus you love him.

Tell someone something nice you saw or heard.

Thank your parents for what they do.

Set the table.

Do not eat candy today.

Make someone happy.

Say something kind to someone.

Clean your room.

Pick up things from the floor.

Do the dishes.

Share something today.

Do neat work in school.

Say a prayer for the sick.

Tell your parents you love them.

Obey in school.

Dust the house.

Pick up your toys.

Dust the house.

Tell your parents you love them.

Play with someone who looks lonely.

Smile at someone.

Be kind today.

Do not watch TV today.

Be kind to someone.

Give up candy or snacks today.

Do you want to be a lamb in Jesus' flock?

Read the verses here.

Ask Jesus to help you live them.

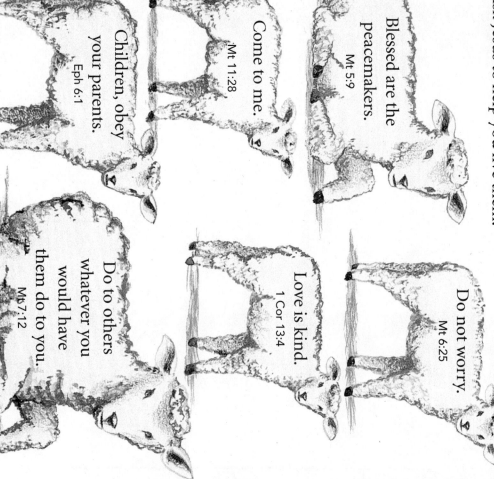

Blessed are the peacemakers.
Mt 5:9

Come to me.
Mt 11:28

Children, obey your parents.
Eph 6:1

Do not worry.
Mt 6:25

Love is kind.
1 Cor 13:4

Do to others whatever you would have them do to you.
Mt 7:12

This book belongs to

_____

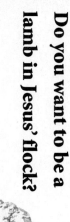

I am the Good Shepherd

John 10:11

Words from the Bible that help me pray . . .

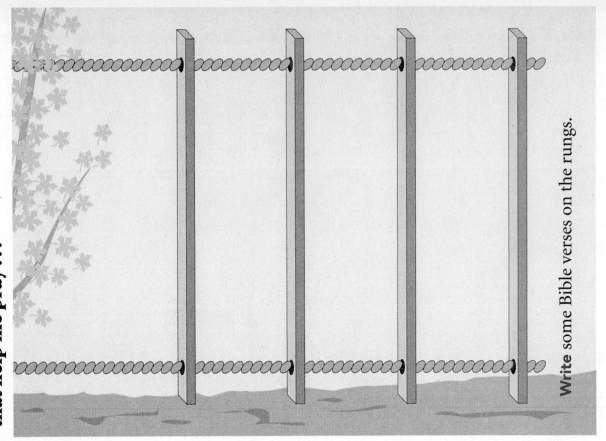

Write some Bible verses on the rungs.

Color a piece of the stained glass every time you use this book.

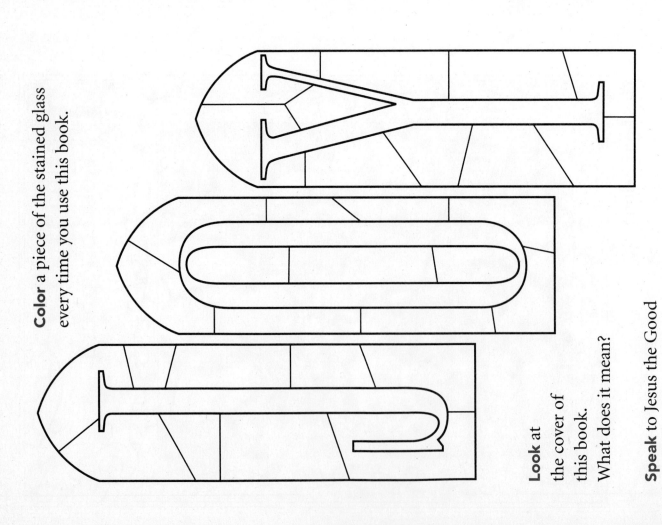

Look at the cover of this book. What does it mean?

Speak to Jesus the Good Shepherd.

Favorite Bible Stories

Draw the pictures. Add your favorite story.

Jesus Cures Someone	Jesus at Sea
Jesus Rises	

Thank Jesus for something he did.

FLOWERS
to pray from...

Do not be afraid.
Mk 5:36

Love one another.
Jn 13:34

Be quiet.
Lk 4:35

Pray to your Father.
Mt 6:6

Keep my commandments.
Jn 14:15

Prayers from the Mass

Do this in memory of me. Lk 22:19

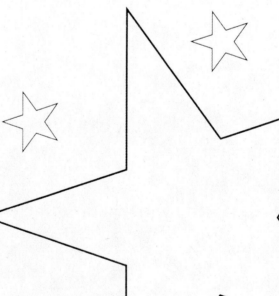

Blessed be God.

Lord, have mercy.

Thanks be to God.

Praise to you, Lord Jesus Christ.

Glory to you, Lord.

Alleluia.

Lift up your hearts.

Let us give thanks.

Lord, I am not worthy.

Go in peace.

You are the **L**ight of the world. Mt 5:14

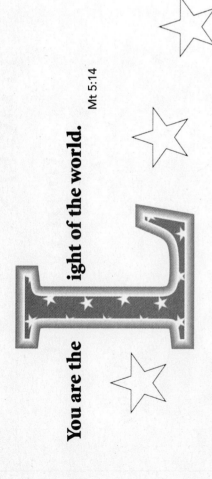

Write inside the star the names of people you want to pray for. Color a star when you pray for one of them.

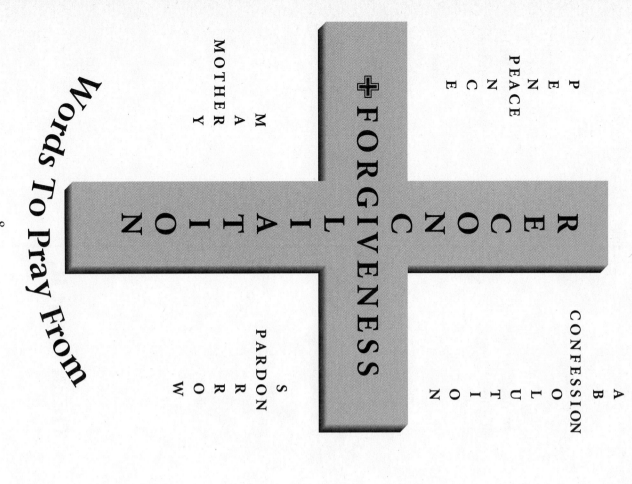

Courage, child, your sins are forgiven.
Mt 9:2

✝ FORGIVENESS

```
P              A
E              B
N   PEACE      CONFESSION
C              O
E              L
               U
               T
               I
               O
               N

        R E C O N C I L I A T I O N

M                    S
A   MOTHER           PARDON
Y                    R
                     R
                     O
                     W
```

Words To Pray From

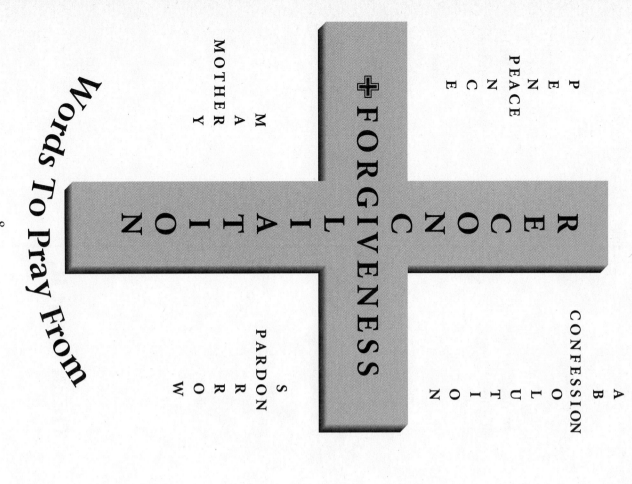

8

O Jesus, I am sorry for the times . . .

I talked back to _____ or _____.

I pouted.

I did not play fair.

I got into a fight.

I gave a hard time to _____.

I was noisy.

I annoyed _____.

I hurt others' feelings.

I was stubborn.

I was selfish.

I did not listen to you, Lord.

A clean heart create
for me, O God.
adapted from Ps 51:12

5

The LORD heard their cry.
Jdt 4:13

You are before me and behind me.
adapted from Ps 139:5

I myself will care for my sheep.
adapted from Ez 34:15

You, LORD, help and comfort me.
Ps 86:17

The LORD gives health and life and blessing.
Sir 34:17

Your hands made me.
Ps 119:73

O God, you have not left those who love you.
adapted from Dn 14:38

The eyes of the LORD watch all things.
adapted from Prv 15:3

The LORD gives wisdom.
Prv 2:5

You are safe.
Tb 12:17

Be happy.
Tb 8:21

The LORD himself gives all good things.
Tb 4:19

Be grateful to the LORD.
Jdt 8:25

You are the God who works wonders.
adapted from Ps 77:15

God indeed is my savior.
Is 12:2

I put my trust in you.
Ps 55:24

over

and

over and

Think about it.

6

7

Fold

My Morning Offering

God, our Father, I offer you today
All I think and do and say.
I offer it with what was done
On earth by Jesus Christ, your Son.

Fold
Back

it
produces
much
fruit.

adapted from
John 12:24

If
a
seed
dies,

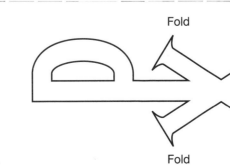

Fold
Back

Fold

Fold

God's Top "Ten"

1. Pray

God's Top "Ten"

3. God's Day

God's Top "Ten"

2. God's Name

God's Top "Ten"

4. Obey

God's Top "Ten"

6.-,9. Pure

God's Top "Ten"

5. Kind

God's Top "Ten"

8. Truthful

God's Top "Ten"

7.-,10. Honest

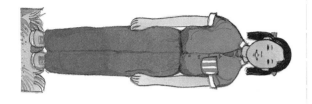

Chapter 7

Cover design by

Chapter 5

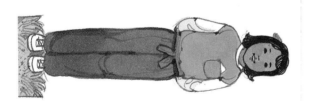

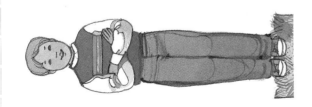

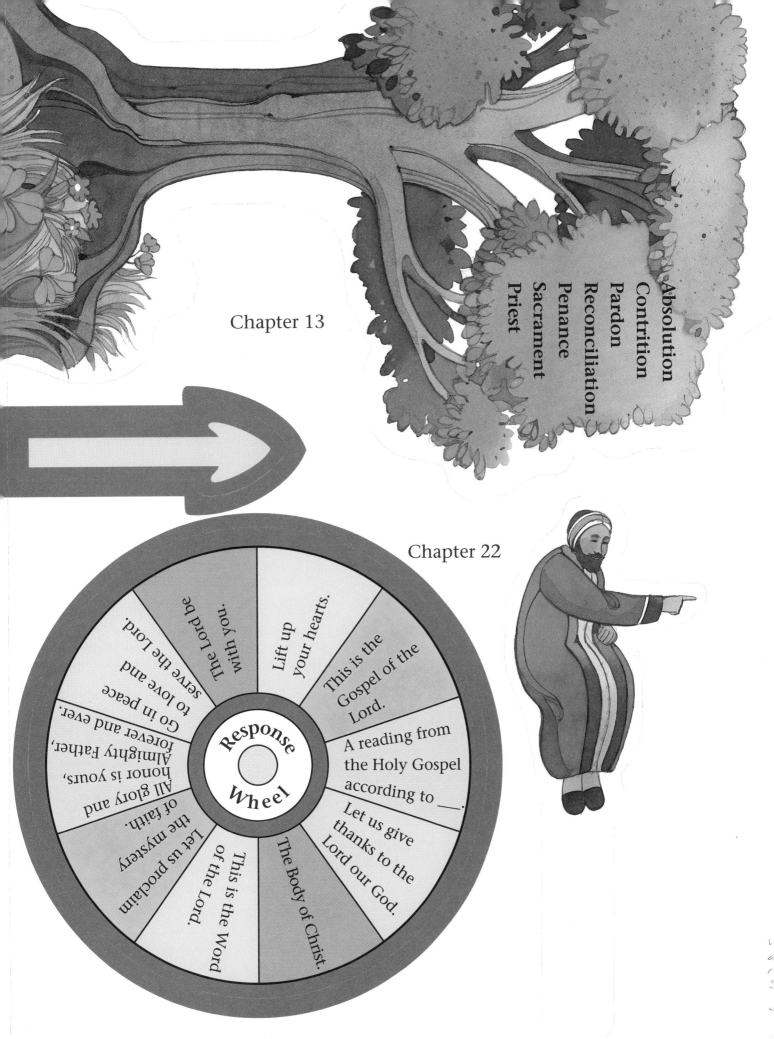

Absolution
Contrition
Pardon
Reconciliation
Penance
Sacrament
Priest

Chapter 13

Chapter 22

Response Wheel

Lift up your hearts.

This is the Gospel of the Lord.

A reading from the Holy Gospel according to ___.

Let us give thanks to the Lord our God.

The Body of Christ.

This is the Word of the Lord.

Let us proclaim the mystery of faith.

All glory and honor is yours, Almighty Father, forever and ever.

Go in peace to love and serve the Lord.

The Lord be with you.